MW00669163

EXCUSE ME!
YOUR ENERGY IS SHOWING

What is Energy and why should you care

WOE —

ONE OF THE GREATEST OF WARRIORS
AND THE MOST MAGNIFICIENT
MASTER TEACHER!
LIVE YOUR LIGHT!

Melissa Mintz

MELISSA MINTZ

Grateful acknowledgement is made to the following for permission to quote from copyrighted material:

Excerpt from "Modulation of DNA conformation by heart-focused intention" by Rollin McCraty, Mike Atkinson, and Dana Tomasino. Copyright © 2003 by HeartMath Research Center. Reprinted by permission of HeartMath Research Center, Institute of HeartMath.

Excerpts from Dying To Be Me: My Journey from Cancer, to Near Death, to True Healing by Anita Moorjani. Copyright © 2012 by Anita Moorjani. Reprinted by permission of Hay House, Inc., Carlsbad, CA.

Published by:
Transformation Books
211 Pauline Drive #513
York, PA 17402
www.TransformationBooks.com

ISBN # 978-1-945252-10-5
Library of Congress Control No: 2016956002

Cover Design: Ranilo Cabo
Layout and typesetting: Ranilo Cabo
Editor: Michelle Cohen
Proofreader: Michelle Cohen
Midwife: Carrie Jareed

Printed in the United States of America

EXCUSE ME!
YOUR ENERGY IS SHOWING

What is Energy and why should you care

TABLE OF CONTENTS

PREFACE

One hot sunny summer day in June of 2003, I decided to go to a bookstore that I had been to on many occasions. Usually, I would go to leisurely browse through the books to see what piqued my interest to purchase, but this day was different. I was heading there with a purpose to buy two copies of Louise Hay's book *You Can Heal Your Life*. I had two people in mind that I was planning on giving the book to as a gift. At the time, it was a very popular book and every metaphysical bookstore I had ever been to had multiple copies. In previous visits, I had seen several copies on the shelf at this store as well, so I knew it would be there.

When I arrived, I saw many cars in the parking lot and expected the bookstore to be crowded. On Saturdays, this place bustled with activity. There were several rooms off the main area of the bookstore where alternative practitioners including healers, psychics, tarot, or astronomy readers saw clients. I walked through the door anticipating seeing a crowd browsing through the books and the small rooms filled with people having a reading or a Reiki session.

Instead, I walked in the bookstore, and the entire place was EMPTY despite the crowded parking lot. As soon as I walked in, an older woman, who stood waiting for me at the door, greeted me.

"Can I help you find something?" she asked me with eager anticipation. I looked at her and what I saw past her startled me. *It's empty*, I thought. *How can it be empty?* There are two people in here: she and I. I was too stunned to answer. It was completely quiet. Dead silence filled the air. I walked past her for a moment and didn't speak. I was surveying the room filled with bookshelves. Then I peeked into the smaller rooms in the store where clients were usually seen. I didn't see the two female owners of the bookstore. They were the ones who always assisted customers and checked out books at the register. The parking lot was full. Where is everyone?!

The lady who waited for me at the door was following me. Letting me look all around. Then finally she spoke. "Is everything okay?" I heard her ask gently. I sensed the concern in her voice.

"Yeah, everything is fine," I replied softly. I could not comprehend what was happening. My logical mind was having a difficult time making sense of all this. *Where are the two ladies who own the place? They're always here!* My mind started to race.

"Is there a book I can help you find?" she asked, as I just stood there in a confused daze.

"Actually, I am looking for the book *You Can Heal Your Life* by Louise Hay. I wanted to purchase two copies."

Without even looking for the book I requested, the lady stood in front of me and said, "We don't have *that* book, but if you are interested in a healing book, I think this book would be of interest to you."

She walked over to the bookcase and efficiently pulled out a book on the shelf. "This is a book called *The Reconnection* by Dr. Eric Pearl," she said as she placed the book in my hands.

The lady was staring at me with great intensity while I looked at the front cover of the book. She was no longer talking. I felt her intense gaze as if she were analyzing my thoughts about this book. She stood just a few inches away from me. I read the jacket cover of the book. We both stood in silence. "This sounds really interesting," I finally said. "I'm going to buy it." I followed her over to the register where she rang up the book. After I walked outside, I saw the parking lot full of cars and the activity of people lingering around and talking.

How strange! Was my recurring thought. *How strange!!* On the drive home, my bewildered mind replayed the scene trying to process everything that happened. The lady was staring at me when I was reading the jacket of the book. I looked up at her. We were standing so close. She did not take her eyes off me. When I looked up, I kept blinking because the light around her was so bright. It was difficult for me to really look at her.

When I walked in, and she greeted me, my first thought was, *That's the brightest woman I have ever seen. She's so bright!* I saw her, standing in front of the bookshelves, watching my every move as I walked around the store.

Her hair was in a stylish short cut with subtle layers, and it glowed. It was red, not Little Orphan Annie red but softer, with hints of auburn. *She has green eyes like myself,* I thought initially when she first greeted me at the door. There was a certain softness revealing wisdom and compassion in her eyes. It seems like a an odd thing to say, but as our eyes met, in that brief moment, this is what I felt.

When I looked at her, I saw light around her. Her radiance was unlike anything I had ever experienced before. It was as if there was a photo shoot, and the photographer put a light behind her to take the picture. So when I looked at her, I saw her glowing in light.

That evening when I got home, I sat in my office and started to read Dr. Eric Pearl's book *The Reconnection, Heal Others, Heal Yourself.* As I was holding the book, I noticed my hands started to tingle like they were falling asleep. I didn't think this was strange and did not attribute this to the book. I just thought my hands were starting to fall asleep. I could not put the book down. I was intrigued and mesmerized and eager to learn more.

INTRODUCTION

Dr. Eric Pearl

Dr. Eric Pearl is recognized as the founder of Reconnective Healing. He is the known instrument for which this frequency was received on the planet. Eric, as he prefers to be called, came up with the phrase Reconnective Healing to differentiate this healing frequency from the other frequencies that are used in various energy healing modalities. I prefer *Energy Medicine Healer* to describe my work. It seems to resonate more with me than the term Reconnective Healer that Eric uses to describe the frequency he is working with and teaching. After all, the *energy* is the *medicine*.

I realize that Eric is doing his work, and I am doing my work. We are both working with the same frequency, but just like any other gift, we are using our innate talent and our unique individualized expressions that are coming through our work, even though we are not directing the healings. Many of us who are doing this work have had a bizarre set of circumstances surrounding how this gift was received into our lives. Eric visited a psychic, who during the reading asked, "What is it that you do?" Eric replied, "I'm a chiropractor." "Oh no," said the psychic, "It's much more than that. Something comes out through your hands, and people receive healings."[1]

All energy healing, whether it is Reiki or Reconnective Healing, is essentially *reconnecting* us back to our source energy. The term Reconnective Healing is a trademark name that defines this specific frequency that people have been trained to work with in Eric's seminars. Dr. Eric Pearl has been traveling all over the world teaching and lecturing about Reconnective Healing.

Recently, I read Eric's book, *The Reconnection,* for the second time. I wanted to re-read this work since I had read it back in June of 2003. I loved this book the first time, and liked it more the second. *The Reconnection* changed my life. One thing that I really respect is Eric's candor and honesty. He doesn't have all the answers. He does not know how this frequency works, and he doesn't pretend to know. When writing a book, most people may feel compelled to come up with a logical explanation for everything as if thinking, *I'm writing a book so I can't just say I don't know all the time.* But Eric wrote, "I don't know," quite a bit throughout his text.[2] For me, this gives him even more credibility.

In the book, Eric talks about how this energy has even been *activated* in people who come to hear his lectures. "I don't know how, when I address larger venues and can only pass through the rows closest to the stage, the people in the balconies and mezzanines start to feel the sensations that indicate the presence of these energies."

Eric talks about how the frequencies seem to transfer through books, CDs, radios, television, magazines, newspapers, etc. How? "I don't know," Eric writes.[3]

As I mentioned previously, when I got home from the bookstore and started reading Eric's book, my hands kept tingling. It was strange and uncomfortable. I kept wondering why my hands were falling asleep. I would shake them awake, and then they would start to tingle again. I never thought to associate this feeling in my hands to the book. This seemed incomprehensible to me.

It was not until I attended the November 2003 seminar to learn Reconnective Healing that Eric talked about people's hands becoming activated from the book. At the completion of the weekend-long training, there was an opportunity for a book signing. I bought another copy of the book there, and Eric signed it. When I hold the signed copy of the book, my hands don't just tingle—I feel them pulse. It's hard to describe, but I feel a much stronger sensation when I hold the book with Eric's signature—more like a throbbing of pulsating energy through my hands. Even now, if I have not held this book for years, I can pick it up on occasion, and it will have the same effect.

I was about a third of the way into reading *The Reconnection* when I realized I wanted to learn how to do this healing. It was as if when reading this book, it jogged a memory buried deep in my subconscious. I was meant to do this work. But it was more than that. I *remembered* I do this work! All the pieces of the puzzle started to unfold before my eyes. *I knew who the lady was who was waiting for me at the bookstore.*

So I Googled Dr. Eric Pearl and found his website. I checked the schedule for the seminar dates and could not believe that in

November he was teaching in Atlanta! This worked out perfectly! Since I was a single mom with two small kids, traveling out of town to a seminar would have been out of the question for me. I saw on the schedule he was teaching Reconnective Healing during a weekend in mid-November and teaching The Reconnection the following weekend. To my delight at the convenience, I registered immediately for both seminars. Somehow, I was very aware that my life would be forever changed. Although, I did not yet comprehend the magnitude of this. I also knew I wanted to meet Eric and learn more about this healing.

SECTION 1

....

ENERGY

Your time is limited, so don't waste it living someone else's life. Don't be trapped by dogma - which is living with the results of other people's thinking. Don't let the noise of others' opinions drown out your own inner voice. And most important, have the courage to follow your heart and intuition.
—Steve Jobs

....

CHAPTER 1

The Journey Begins

It is good to have an end to journey toward;
but it is the journey that matters, in the end.
—Ernest Hemingway

The Training

Before I knew it, it was already November and the start of my much anticipated Reconnective training. The Reconnective Healing seminar began on a Friday evening with a presentation from Dr. Eric Pearl, who shared his fascinating journey of how he became a healer. Saturday and Sunday were the hands-on healing training. At the end of the day on Sunday, we were given a certificate of completion.

The following weekend was the start of The Reconnection training. I found out during the training class that is it very unusual to schedule the weekend seminars for Reconnective Healing and The Reconnection back to back. For me, this was further validation that I was meant to be here. During the seminar, Eric explained, "I just really like Atlanta and wanted to spend more time here."

"For those of you who will be in The Reconnection training next weekend, you will need to be reconnected before the seminar," Eric announced as people were rushing around picking up their notes and folders from the training to leave for their respective hometowns. The majority of the people had driven in from the surrounding Southern states or had flown in for this from even greater distances. I was one of only a handful of students who live here in Atlanta.

I wasn't exactly sure what The Reconnection actually was, but I was certain that I wanted to learn how to do this so I could offer this service to my clients in addition to the healing session. At this time, all I understood was that The Reconnection was done in two sessions, and we were going to learn how to "draw lines" on a person's body to connect them to the universal energy grid of light and information.

What?!!! *Why do I have to be reconnected to learn The Reconnection?* I started to feel a little panicky. Completing this training was really important to me. How was I going to find a practitioner in the next day? This meant that I had one week to find someone who was trained in The Reconnection and have both sessions completed. I did not know any Reconnective Practitioners in Atlanta. Besides, not everyone who completes the Reconnective Healing has done the additional training to facilitate The Reconnection, which makes this task even more daunting.

I remembered Eric saying they were all staying in town the entire week. There were several teaching assistants, but I had already met Doug Devito during our breakouts when we did the exercises to practice connecting with the energy. I caught a glimpse of him on the other side of the room and darted over. "Doug, will you reconnect me?" I asked while trying to catch my breath. "I'm taking the seminar next weekend."

To my relief, Doug agreed, and we set up a day mid-week for the first session. I still had to pay The Reconnection fee like any other client. The fee for the two sessions is $333.00. According to Eric, the information for the exact fee was given to him during a channeling session. This is the vibration for the energy exchange. This is the fee that all certified Reconnective Healers agree to charge for The Reconnection.

Since we did not have a massage table in the hotel room, Doug instructed me to lie across the end of the bed. After only a few minutes into the session, my toes were moving. Not just randomly moving, but in a constant synchronized succession. It is a little difficult to explain. My little toe on my left foot started moving, then the adjacent toe, then the next toe, and so forth. Then my right big toe would move. The adjacent toes moved until it reached the little toe on my right foot, then back to the little toe on my left foot. The best way to describe this: it seemed as though my toes were doing "the wave." This was non-stop for the entire forty-minute session.

My toes were moving—one toe after the other, similar to keys being played on a keyboard, striking keys one through ten, then starting back at one. There were no pauses of energy from one foot to the other, just constant motion. I could feel each toe moving back and forth—with such power! My toes felt like they were going to fall off.

If this wasn't uncomfortable and peculiar enough, I also had to deal with a wave of energy traveling over my toes. I actually felt a wave as my toes were doing "the wave." Yes, I know this may sound confusing, but there were two bizarre issues going on: feeling the wave of energy; and, simultaneously, each toe physically moving up and down performing "the wave."

To say it was very uncomfortable is putting it mildly. Halfway through the session I started to feel exhausted and worn out. I kept thinking over and over during the entire session, *I don't know how much more of this I can take.* It was close to being unbearable. I could not wait for the session to end.

The force of the wave traveling over my toes as they individually and powerfully moved up and down was, at that time, the strangest experience I have ever perceived. During the session, I was continually thinking, *Doug must be freaking out over "my freaky toes"!* I wondered why Doug didn't seem to be concerned or mention how wildly my toes were moving during the forty-minute session. *I guess he doesn't want to disturb me,* I thought, a little surprised that he did not ask if he should stop.

The power of the energy was wearing me down. When Doug tapped me on my right collarbone and gently said, "I'm finished," I could not have been happier. *Thank God that's over,* I silently said. I opened my eyes and looked around the room in a dazed relaxation. Still lying on the edge of the bed, not yet ready to get up, I felt a peacefulness that was not present during the session. My eyes focused now on Doug, who was standing on the side of the bed.

"Did you see my freaky toes?!"

Weird to Freaky to ... *What??*

"Doug! Did you see my freaky toes?!" I yelled again, no longer able to contain my excitement. After all, I had been waiting for the session to end so we could finally talk about my freaky toes! Doug did not respond. He just stared at me. This was certainly not the reaction I anticipated. I could tell he did not know what to say. *Why is he not talking to me about the toes?* I thought he probably could not wait to discuss this as well.

"My toes! You didn't see them moving?" I said now a little calmer.

"Your toes weren't moving."

To this day, I can still hear Doug's reply in my head as if no time had passed. I sat up and moved off the bed to the chair in the room. "Doug," I said, so startled. "You didn't see my toes moving?"

"I saw your toes during the session, and they did not move." I had taken off my shoes and socks before the session, so my feet were visible for him to see.

I explained my freaky toes during the session and the wave of energy over my toes and the force at which each one was moving. "Doug, during the session, I kept thinking about how you must be freaking out over my freaky toes! I even wondered why you didn't mention this during the session because it was so bizarre."

How can this be explained? Who knows really? This was real. My toes were moving. The power of the wave of energy traveling from left to right simultaneously over my toes was real, too. I am not going to try to explain the unexplainable. Some things we are never going to fully comprehend. I decided this is one of those experiences where I am going to accept that not everything in this world can be understood and explained.

Doug was not at all fazed by what I had experienced during the session. He did not think I was crazy because I experienced my toes moving, but not visibly moving. He was used to weird. He and Eric were working with this energy every day and traveling around the world teaching. Along the way, they experienced and heard about many bizarre and strange events. *In their world, the abnormal was the normal.*

The Reconnection Continues

I would describe the second session of The Reconnection the following day as "uneventful." This session was very different from the previous day; it felt like a very relaxing day at the spa. I did not experience anything unusual at all. It was just peaceful and enjoyable.

The Reconnection training the following weekend was intense. There was a lot of information to remember. I wondered if the reason we needed to be reconnected before this training was that being reconnected back to the universal intelligence might help us to remember all this stuff.

In addition to learning the activation points on the body, we also learned about the meridian lines, sometimes called acupuncture lines. These meridian lines on the body act as an *energy highway* to allow the energy to flow smoothly and freely without obstruction. Just as a traffic jam creates a blockage when you drive on the road, an energy jam will cause the same problem: slow movement.

Originally, these energy lines on our bodies continued out and connected us with the grid lines of the entire Universe, but over time we became disconnected from this source energy. What does all this really mean? For a simple explanation, think of our bodies originally being connected to a high-speed Internet. We could download information and process it very quickly. Then one day the Internet connection no longer worked, and we felt "unplugged" without having access to the intelligence of the cosmos.

The Reconnection is about our reconnecting once again to the vast universal energy grid, which allows us to communicate better with the universal intelligence. During the session, we draw new energy lines on the body to reconnect one back to the universal grid of energy. This is more of a gradual download that occurs for the remainder of your life. Just think what would happen if your electronic devices had a sudden surge of energy. They would blow out. This is why we have surge protectors. Our nervous system, as well, would not be able to handle the expanded amount of light and information if this were an instantaneous download.

What are the benefits of receiving this influx of light and information? This is a personal transformation on a physical, mental, and spiritual level. I use the term personal because everyone's experience is personalized. The actual session experience will vary from person to person just as a healing session will have a unique experience for the individual. At any time when we connect with the energy, it is reacting differently for each person. This is the Universal Energy working in tandem with your higher self for the appropriate experience to take place. Some of the benefits to being reconnected back to the universal energy grid may include awakening to your life purpose, higher intuition, and a spiritual transformation.

My clients seem to be confused with the difference between a Reconnective Healing session and The Reconnection. The main difference is the *intent* for the session. A healing session is just that:

the intention to channel energy for the appropriate healing to take place. During The Reconnection, it is certainly possible for healing to take place since this is another opportunity to participate with the energy, but the intention of the session is so we may once again be "plugged in" to this vast communication network to accelerate our spiritual growth and human evolution.

I can honestly say being reconnected back to the universal energy grid is one of the best gifts I have ever given myself. During the first day with Doug during my freaky toe session, I intuitively knew I was being shown the power of this energy. I have never experienced anything like that before; such power and force pulsated throughout my body to the point I was feeling worn out. Once I started facilitating sessions with actual clients, I experienced this again.

There was one time in particular where I was facilitating a distance healing for a client who resided outside of Georgia. I was standing in my healing room that I have located in my house with my hands over the massage table as if the client were physically present and lying on the table. I focused my attention on my hands, and when the familiar tingling and pulsing sensation was present, I started moving my hands—hovering above the distance client playing in their energy field. After just a few moments, the energy kept growing, not just in my hands and arms, but pulsating throughout my body with such force that I could no longer stand. My body could not contain this incredible surge of power. I facilitated the rest of the session lying on my back on the carpet in the healing room and directing the energy for the distance client.

That particular healing was actually the last time that occurred. I seemed to be able to master directing and controlling the flow of energy so that this has never happened again. *How did I do this? Who knows!?* This seemed to be a recurring theme. Things just started to happen. Gifts that I did know that I had started to express themselves. This became my new life, where the abnormal didn't seem that abnormal anymore. Although I have shared a part of my experience during The Reconnection, everyone's experience will be different. The client will have the appropriate experience take place for them at that particular time in their life.

Not everything that happens is always as it appears to be. What I mean is—there is the *seen* taking place and the *unseen* taking place. I can sense and feel when I am working with a client that a spirit guide or the angelic realm may be present during the session. I have had particular clients where I have thought, *It's so crowded in here*, as I felt the presence of guides, angels, archangels, and masters. I refer to these beings a their *light team*. It's as if a whole team of spirit beings is present to assist and guide the session for the best outcome possible for the individual based on their particular life plan for this incarnation.

How Did This Become MY Life?

I have days where I think to myself, *How did this become my life? I used to be so normal!* This wasn't supposed to be my life. I had another plan, and I don't recall working with energy as one of my career goals.

I certainly did not grow up thinking, *One day I would like to channel energy through my hands.* I was always drawn to healing as a kid, but in my mind, this inner calling meant medical school. So, I prepared for this unwavering desire. I finished my pre-med at Ohio State. After that, I transferred to a small private college and received a Bachelor of Science in Nuclear Medicine. After many years of school, studying, and working in the hospital setting, I realized that medical school no longer felt right for me.

I decided to work in the medical industry and accepted a position with a pharmaceutical company. I have worked in the pharmaceutical/biotech industry for my entire career in several different positions of sales and management. I still work in the biotech industry as a Neurology Clinical Consultant. I have thirty years' experience working in oncology, neurology, psychiatry, and immunology throughout my sales career. My extensive knowledge of the medical field and healthcare industry, in addition to my innate spiritual gifts, has given me a unique insight and greater perspective of conventional and alternative healing modalities, which comes through in my writing.

When I completed the two weekend seminars in November of 2003, my daughter Morgan and my son Brandon were eight and nine years old respectively. They still refer to this time period as "when Mom got weird." When they would call me from the nurse's office and say, "Pick me up from school. I'm sick." I would answer, "Go back to class. I'll do a distance healing on you."

"Don't tell anyone you're a healer," they would say. "The kids on the bus already ask us why you walk the dog with the parrot on your shoulder."

"I've told you why. He poops on my head."

"Please don't!" They would plead with me. "You'll seem even weirder!!"

As time went on, their attitude slowly started to change. No . . . not the "you are weird" part. They still think I am the strangest person they know, and they mention this a little too frequently. They still tell me to "just talk normal" when we are around their friends, as if I may slip up and say to one of them, "Wow, you have the most beautiful energy!"

What changed is that they were able to experience this energy. They could actually feel the energy during a session. This became real to them even if they still did not understand how energy could heal. I get it. Many people are new to this concept, hence the reason why I decided to write this book. My purpose of creating *Excuse Me! Your Energy is Showing* is to educate people about energy in all forms, not just healing energy. Energy is everywhere and in all things, and this is not going to change. If you think this book is just about ENERGY, you would be mistaken. This is a book about LIFE. *Energy is the foundation of every aspect of our life.* Everything that is, and has ever been in existence, is energy. This is what I write about.

My entire family, who initially thought I was "whacked out of my mind," (their exact words) now beg me to work on them (and their pets) because they have experienced firsthand these unexplained miracles start to unfold.

One synchronistic event after another seemed to catapult me into this modality of healing work. I saw an entirely new life unfold for me that I had never even considered before, or thought possible for that matter.

CHAPTER 2

Your Energy Is Showing

The best and most beautiful things in the world cannot be seen or even touched—they must be felt with the heart.
—Helen Keller

"So . . . you're an Energy Medicine Healer? How do you heal? With energy?!? Where do you get the energy from?"

This is the usual beginning dialogue whenever I am speaking to a potential client about the work that I do. It does not matter if I am talking to someone on the phone, at a health fair, or out at the local bar. No one seems to comprehend where the energy comes from. Why? Because the explanation is just too simple. People don't get simple. We tend to think there has to be something more to it and do not want to accept a simplified explanation. Most people have a greater grasp of the equation E = mc2 than they do of Energy; that is—Universal Energy.

Albert Einstein was a brilliant physicist who discovered the theory of relativity (E = mc2). His discovery showed that energy and matter are actually two different forms of the same thing. Albert Einstein discovered that Energy = **matter**. You can think of this equation as a formula for how much energy we need to create the appearance of matter.

I see and comprehend the world as energy; so, to me, this is an easy concept to understand. We are energy. Our world is energy. We try to over-complicate things and make easy concepts more difficult to understand. Our bodies readily respond to the energy being introduced because it *recognizes* the energy. This is the essence of who we really are: *Energy Beings.*

"Where do you get the energy from?" The question is repeated, and I finally respond, "From the energy that is all around us." As the person starts looking around them for any signs of the energy, I continue with, "Our world is energy. I focus my attention on this energy and channel it through my hands." Then I get *the look*. It's the all too familiar "you're an idiot" look my teenage children give me whenever I speak.

Universal Energy

Universal Energy is the energy all around us. Because we don't *see* the energy, it can be difficult for people to grasp something intangible. We don't see radio waves, but we know that they are there. We don't see frequency, but we know things can vibrate at different frequencies. Energy is not intangible. Energy is alive. Energy is palpable. We can *feel* energy.

Universal Energy is the base energy from which everything is derived—the plants, flowers, trees, rocks, animals, mountains, oceans, and everything else you can think of. Universal Energy is the basic structure of everything: the Earth, sun, moon, and stars. If you think of everything in existence from the billions of galaxies to the vast, infinite Universe comprised of Universal Energy, you would be correct. We, the human species, are Universal Energy. This is our essence. This is the essence of all things. So, you may ask yourself, if Universal Energy is in all things, how did it get here?

Universal Energy is the source energy from our Creator, and it has always been here. There was no beginning and no end. It just was. This source energy from our Creator has always been in existence, just as our Creator has always been in existence. If Universal Energy is from our Creator, and our Creator is infinite—then Universal Energy is infinite.

Because the energy from our Creator, or Source, is the essence of everything in existence, many healers (including myself) may refer to energy using interchangeable words such as Love, Light, Consciousness, Source, or Creator. All of these words are sometimes used to describe God.

Everything in Existence Vibrates

We are all *vibrating beings* who live in a *vibrating Universe.* Vibration is a term used to describe movement. Energy is constantly moving: energy vibrates. Everything has its own unique signature vibration. Plants, animals, rocks, dirt, even our food and water, have a vibration. This vibration has a corresponding frequency. The faster something vibrates, the higher the frequency. A slower vibration corresponds to a lower frequency.

Our thoughts and emotions are energy too and have a corresponding vibration. Emotions such as fear and hate are of a low vibration (slow) and are associated with a low frequency. Lower vibrational energy is very dense. Think of water molecules moving slower to form ice. Love and gratitude are of the highest vibration (fast) and have a corresponding high frequency. Higher vibrational energy is much lighter. Think of water molecules moving faster to create steam. Our thoughts and emotions certainly affect whether we are vibrating at a higher or lower frequency.

Did you know the words we speak are very powerful? These words are real energy and vibrate as well. Now that you have a better understanding that feelings and emotions carry an energy and vibration, just think how much more power your words have when coupled with intense emotion and feeling. It's not just what we say; it's how we say it! Words do have great power, and the feeling and intensity of the emotion are felt and received by another person.

Everything in Existence is Energy. The essence of who we are is energy. *We are walking, talking, thinking energy fields.* We spread our energy wherever we go with whomever we meet. Everything on the planet vibrates and affects and alters the vibration of everything in existence.

You've Got a Groovy "Vibe"

Who remembers the '60s? Some of you who lived then may not even remember them. In the 1960s during the era of free love and the "hippie generation," we often heard the word "vibe." This was the generation of young people who celebrated peace, love, and freedom. These "hippies" used the word *vibe* as slang for *vibration* in expressions like, "Hey, man . . . that guy had a really good vibe," and "I knew I shouldn't have trusted him; I didn't like his vibe."

Early on, this hippie movement was more of a spiritual awakening. It was a period when young people got together sharing a common bond to create a lifestyle of personal freedom, expression of love, and a peaceful world. Hippies were usually more in tune with the energy of others around them because they placed more of a focused attention on consciously getting a read on another's energy. When walking into a room, there was a sense of feeling the vibe of the people present. The energy was a good vibe with a feeling of warm, loving, and peaceful people or a bad vibe with people of lesser intentions of judgment, greed, and hatred. The room may also have been filled with people wearing bell-bottoms, listening to psychedelic rock while smoking weed from a bong, but that's not the point.

What I am saying is, we are all aware of the energy around us. Even though the energy is invisible, we still *perceive* the energy. Have you ever walked into a place, whether it be a restaurant or a bar, and thought, *It just doesn't feel right* and left? You are perceiving the energy in the room. We can *feel* the energy. Some people notice energy on a more conscious level than others; that's all.

Are You Frequency Friends?

We have all, at one time or another, met someone that we did not like right away. Maybe we met someone that we immediately did not trust and were unsure why. This is experiencing another person's energy. We can sense what they are like in a matter of a few seconds.

We can feel and connect with another person's energy field. We aren't trying to do this—we just do it, naturally and subconsciously. Conversely, we have all met someone that we immediately really liked and connected with. Again, we felt their energy on a subconscious level. We connected with someone whose energy and vibration was similar to our own. We liked their vibe.

Even if you are not consciously aware of this, whenever you are around other people there is an energy exchange. The entire world is based on energy transference. Energy is always moving and flowing; it does not remain stagnant. Every place you go, you are radiating energy. You are broadcasting who you are in every moment of your existence. *Everywhere you go, you are announcing yourself to the Universe.* Everything you come into contact with changes in response to your energy. Whether you are in a large room or one-on-one with another person.

You are a walking, talking antennae who is transmitting and receiving frequency.

When you are around other people, your energy is altered. Have you ever noticed that your behavior is different around different people? Did you ever wonder why your personality changes when you are around one person and different around another? We have said before, "This person brings out the best in me." We are reacting to their energy, even if we do this subconsciously. When we are around certain people, we feel loved and uplifted and happy. Around other people, we may feel distressed and irritable, and can't wait to get away from them. We are reacting to their vibration, which determines the frequency they are radiating.

A mental exercise you can do to determine how you feel about the people that are in your life is take out a piece of paper and write down their names. Now think about how you feel when you are around each person. Place a happy face or a frown by their name; or place a check mark, star, dot, whatever you prefer. The point of this is to create a new habit of being more consciously aware of who you spend your time with and being in healthy, loving and supportive friendships and relationships. After doing this exercise one or two times, you will do this naturally in your mind, by just thinking about a person and noticing your emotions.

Spend time with the people who are on the happy face list. As you become more aware of how your energy flows when you are around other people, you will mindfully seek out *frequency friends* who seem to have a similar awareness and energy. Now that I am more aware of how my energy flows and how I feel around certain people, I seek out others with whom I feel more of a spiritual connection.

I try to avoid people who I do not enjoy being around. I am one of these people that would rather spend time by myself doing things I enjoy doing than be around someone I don't really want to spend time with. It's okay to spend time by ourselves. Sometimes, we may feel like we always have to be around other people. I prefer to spend time with people who are positive and trying to make a difference in the world. In the past, it didn't bother me if people did not support my healing work and my writing, or thought I was whacked out my mind if I talked about either. That's okay. People have their own beliefs. I still feel that way, but I choose to surround myself with friends who do support me, and I feel comfortable enough that I can be myself. These are my *frequency friends*. You could say that we are on a more similar wavelength.

Frequency Group

When you start doing this on a more conscious level, you will naturally make more of an effort to spend time with the people who you feel more of a frequency match. This is your *frequency group*. The people you migrate to and enjoy spending time with. The friends you feel happy around and can laugh and have fun and feel at ease. This is why sometimes you will make up excuses to avoid spending time with people you know who are negative, angry, and irritable. You become them: negative, angry, and irritable.

You know who these people are; you don't want to answer the phone when they call. You make plans to do things with them, only to feel a sense of dread and uneasiness as the planned outing is approaching. It's not that these people are bad or evil, and you should run for the hills. The issue is that as you grow and continue to become more aware, you have a shift in consciousness. When we have a shift in consciousness, our vibration also shifts and becomes higher. We have a greater awareness. When we change our vibration, we change our frequency.

Vibration Change = Frequency Change

This is why over time many friendships seem to dissolve. Not all friendships are meant to last a lifetime. We are constantly changing. This is normal and part of our spiritual growth. Sometimes, we just outgrow people. As we evolve, our vibration changes as well. You cannot force someone to increase their vibration. Not everyone will awaken at the same time. You may outgrow a friend on a different path and may not desire to spend as much time with this person as you had in the past.

Every one of us will awaken and grow and evolve on our own timeline. It cannot be forced.

Does this mean you should leave your husband or wife if you feel that they are not on the exact same path as you or hold all the same beliefs as you? Of course not. No one is on the exact same path and has the exact same way of thinking. If you are at a higher vibration, you may be assisting your partner in their spiritual growth. If it is time for any type of relationship to dissolve, you will know this by how you feel around another person. Are you happy, or do you feel anxious and depressed? Do you feel loved and supported? Do you love this person? Do you feel good about yourself in this relationship? Can you grow in this relationship? Do you feel drained from all their drama!? *Do you often feel more like a therapist than a friend?*

I think many of us have or had friendships like this where we got so caught up with the drama queens. Their constant complaining will drain your time and energy for advice, but they will rarely make any change in their life to move forward. You end up having the same conversation over and over and over. After awhile, you will inevitably realize this type of friendship is a major frustration as these people are such an energy drain. You know it. You feel it. The *energy vampires* are sucking your energy right out of you. Don't be their next victim.

Oftentimes, we will try to use logic to rationalize in our minds reasons to stay or leave a relationship. Honor your feelings. *Your feelings are your truth.*

You Think You Are a Healer?

"Where did you learn to do this?" is another question I hear frequently. "I read a book and went to a seminar."

"You went to a seminar, and now you think you're a healer!??" someone asked during a phone consultation. I use the word "asked" politely. Actually, the caller screamed this at me in total disgust.

Hahahahahahahaha. . . . I always laugh at this. It's like saying to a doctor, you went to medical school, and now you think you are a doctor! You went to cooking school, and now you think you are a chef! You went to heating and air school, and now you think you can work on my air-conditioner.

You went to nursing school, and you think you are a nurse. You took a class, and you think you are a psychic. You went to massage school, and now you think you can give me a massage. You have a teaching degree and. . . .

All right! All right! I know. Enough already. But you see where I am going with this. We have training for almost anything we do in life, whether it is playing the guitar or learning how to draw and paint, to the rigorous, intensive training to become a world-renowned heart surgeon. Even if a person has a natural ability at something, we still work to refine and enhance these skills, whether it is a formalized training program or our own self-study.

Our innate gifts and talents still come through in the work that we do even though we have specialized training for various things. Of course, this happens. This is why no two people are ever the exact same at anything they do. You could have two surgeons who had a similar GPA in medical school, attended the same fellowship program, and yet one is a gifted surgeon while the other is barely average. Or look at it this way: several students took swimming lessons for years from the same swim coach. They were all on the same swim team. The swimmers attended the same number of practices. One of the students is Michael Phelps. The rest now swim as a hobby or enjoy lounging around their neighborhood pool. Different levels of skill, expertise, and par excellence come through in everything that we do.

"How did you become a healer?" is a recurring question I hear whenever I mention the energy work that I do. I have always answered, "I came across a book about healing and went to a seminar." The answer was short and succinct and seemed to satisfy the curiosity of the person asking the question. Now, you who are reading this book will know the truth. The answer is even shorter with simply, "An Angel was waiting for me at a bookstore."

CHAPTER 3

Gifts *Are* Gifts

Our talents are the gift that God gives to us . . .
What we make of our talents is our gift back to God.
—Leo Buscaglia

I sometimes think about that afternoon back in June of 2003 at the bookstore. I wonder if I would have been as confident in my work if the book came to me in a different way. What if I had borrowed the book from a friend? I could have heard about it from someone and ordered it through Amazon, but this was not how the situation played out. An Angel stood at the door waiting for me and placed Eric's book in my hand. This is where my initial confidence came from. Otherwise, I probably would have been more skeptical of my ability and wondered how I could facilitate healings with the same results as Eric. I was just an ordinary person who had a sales job by day. I didn't think of myself as overly spiritual. I had not taken any other workshops or learned any other type of healing modality as many others had done who were in my training class.

I received the book *The Reconnection* on that day because I was *ready to receive* that book on that day. I believe that the gifts that we have will express themselves more fully when we are ready to receive them.

We Are All Healers

All human beings have this gift. We are *all* healers. Every single person on this planet has the capacity to heal. *We are born with the capacity to self-heal and to heal others.* This is our birthright. This is our innate gift. Our true essence is pure light. We are all created from divine light, which is the frequency of love. The highest vibration in existence is the vibration of LOVE. We spend our lives seeking it. Why do you think we all want love? Because our essence is pure love. This is who we are.

Our pure essence is the frequency of love and light. We spend our lives seeking our innate God Force of love and light.

We all need love to survive and thrive. Because all human beings are of divine light, we are created with a vibrational quality where it is possible to create the higher vibration of harmony and love. **This is the healing frequency of pure love and light.** This is the vibration that is in alignment with our true essence, our true self. This is our source energy. This is the energy from our Creator. Remember, as I have mentioned in the previous chapter, it is this source energy—this Universal Energy—that we use to heal. This is why some people may use the word *Light* or *Love* as well to describe God.

The healing vibration ultimately is creating peace, harmony, and balance within us.

Well . . . wait a minute. What if someone is a serial killer? Do they have the capacity to heal? What if someone is an atheist? Can they become a healer? Again, as described above, since our pure essence is created from divine light, we all have the capacity to heal. With that being said, only certain individuals are drawn to become healers and desire to create a *reconnection back to our source energy:* divine light.

Even though all human beings are of a vibrational quality where they can take themselves into alignment with their true self, there are only certain individuals who are drawn to receive a reconnection back to our source energy of pure love and light. *That's what all the modalities of healing do.* When we connect with this energy, we create a reconnection back to our source energy: this divine light from God. This is the foundation of all healing procedures, regardless of the technique used. Healing treatments may appear to be very different in nature. Some types of healing may appear complex and dramatic. Other methods such as sound healing may appear to be simple. It is our perception of these healing options and understanding of them that determines how we view them.

Why are there different healing styles to choose from? There are many different treatment options to choose from because we each perceive the Universe differently. Our world is full of people with varying levels of awareness. This is why we have many different choices of healing.

One individual will view the Universe from a certain point of view and create an entire healing modality out of it.

This is why one type of healing may resonate with you more than another because of your present awareness at that point of time. One healing method may feel more appropriate to you at that time in your life. As your awareness changes, another type of healing may feel more appropriate.

All the different energy healing options may look different, but essentially the end result is the same. Energy healing works by creating a reconnection of divine light (our source energy) to our physical, mental, emotional, and spiritual bodies.

Are You Visible?

Sometimes it seems that people who are famous just come out of nowhere. I remember when I first saw Oprah on *The Oprah Winfrey Show*. My first thought was, *Where did she come from?* My second thought was, *How did she get her own talk show?* It seemed like all of a sudden she just vaporized on the television screen and was a famous talk show host.

Famous athletes do not "just appear" either. Do you think Michael Phelps made his first appearance as a swimmer in the Olympics? Of course not. He had been preparing for that moment since he was a little kid, learning to swim on a swim team and honing his skills.

People don't just come out of nowhere. It just seems like they do. When we see a new actor in a major motion picture, it may seem as though he just starred in his first acting role since we did not know who he was. The likely scenario is that this actor had been acting for years. He was probably working on his craft since he was a kid, taking acting classes, attending a performing arts college, working in local theater, small television parts, for possibly ten or more years.

So what changed? *The visibility changed.* That's all. People become visible. It is this new visibility that creates "celebrity status." This is why once someone is on a reality television show, they become famous. These people are now "stars" of their own "reality." It does not matter that they have never done any acting before. It doesn't even matter that they have no "talent" to speak of. What matters? They are now visible. People know who they are. This is why we have overnight fame.

I am still trying to comprehend how people can be stars of their own reality. I think it is so funny when I hear someone being introduced on a television show as a "Reality TV Star." I have a reality too!! Doesn't anyone care about my reality? I guess not. . . .

Most of the time, the gifts that we come into this lifetime with will present themselves at an early age. We may not acknowledge them yet or even realize this was a gift that will be a significant part of our life until much later when we are older. Oprah is a great example of this:

Oprah was able to read and write before the age of three. Did you know Oprah skipped kindergarten because she wrote a note to her teacher on the first day of school stating she should be in the first grade? Her teacher agreed. She was moved to the first grade. The following year she skipped second and started third grade. Oprah's gift of persuasive communication was already expressing itself at a very early age. She continued to develop this gift throughout her childhood. She won a scholarship to Tennessee State where she majored in Speech Communications and Performing Arts. Oprah won the grand prize of $1000 in the Elks Club speech contest. This was the title of her winning speech: *The Negro, the Constitution, and the United States.*

As with all gifts, it still takes commitment, determination, and passion to develop what is already there.

Look at all the people who are successful at what they do. They put many hours of time and effort into developing their gifts, even if what they are doing looks effortless. Gifted people do not just appear out of nowhere; they just become more visible in the public eye.

People move from obscurity to visibility and often back to obscurity. The media has a lot to do with this. When people see someone on television all of a sudden, they become a *visible public figure* even if they have been doing the work for many years.

Do you think Dr. Oz just came out of nowhere? He had been practicing medicine for years and years. He just became more *visible* through television appearances.

Our Gifts Are Spiritual Gifts

We all have innate gifts. This is true for anything we do. No matter what we choose to do in life, we all have varying skill sets and abilities. This holds true for everything we do. I am not only referring to metaphysical gifts with healers, psychics, and tarot readers. We see varying levels of abilities in sports, music, art, singers, dancers, doctors, lawyers, accountants, etc.

All of our gifts are spiritual gifts. They all come from God. No matter what you do, even if you are a housewife or a student, each of us has individual gifts. We are all unique. There is no comparison between one person to another. We are all here to be of service to each other. We are here to share our innate gifts and talents.

As I had previously mentioned, even though Eric taught me Reconnective Healing, I realized early on that Eric is doing his work, and I am doing my work. What I mean is: *there are no two people doing the exact same work in anything.* No matter what we do in life, we are all bringing our own innate talents and gifts. We bring to our work the gifts that we have developed in this lifetime and also the gifts that we incarnate with that have been honed and developed in our past lifetimes. Whether you believe in past lives or not, it still does not change the fact that no two people are alike, and all of us bring our unique individualized expression to our work.

Reading *The Reconnection* jogged a memory within me that I do this work. *I remembered that I was meant to do this work again.* Certainly, my confidence as a healer grew as I completed the formalized training. The Reconnective Healing seminar provided the necessary foundation that I needed at the time. But for me, it was just that—a foundation upon which my innate gifts became stronger.

CHAPTER 4

Is This All Real?

Whether you think you can or think you can't, you're right.
—*Henry Ford*

Why Are You Here?

There was an event that has always stood out in my mind during my Reconnective Healing training in the first weekend seminar in November. We broke out into groups of four people to practice working with the energy. This entailed just playing around with feeling the energy. One person would lie on the massage table, then the three of us would hover our hands above the person connecting with their energy. After about fifteen minutes, we would rotate and another would get a turn on the table.

There was a girl in my foursome who said to me, "What qualifies you to be here?" I did not reply. I just stared at her. I didn't understand what she meant. After realizing I was not going to answer, she clarified with, "I don't mean you're not qualified to be here. I just mean . . . what else have you done?" Again, I did not answer. I was too shocked to come up with a response. I thought, *Why is she asking me this?* First of all, I have not done anything like this before.

She filled in the awkward silence. "I am an ordained minister. I have been trained in Reiki and EFT, and I am in the works of having a television series about my work . . . kind of like what James Van Praagh did." There were a few other certifications and titles that she rambled on about that I have forgotten. She said she would be on some public broadcasting channel soon. After realizing she was stuck with me for the next few hours in our foursome, she finally said, "You must read a lot . . . right? Do you read any metaphysical books?"

"Yes," I replied with a sigh of relief. "I read." This seemed to suffice that in her mind I was possibly a tad worthy to have bestowed upon me the gift of healing, and she finally ceased her interrogation.

I actually felt as though I had an advantage that I did not train in any other type of healing. Some of my fellow students were chiropractors, Reiki Masters, and other healthcare practitioners. Because I was not trained in any other technique, I didn't worry about what to do with my hands. The people who were trained in other healing modalities had a more difficult time accepting that we just "play with the energy" and thought there has to be more to it than this.

Also, since I was not trained in Reiki or another energy healing, I did not have to worry about the interference of other frequencies. When I felt the frequency as tingling or heat or pulsing in my hands, I knew it was The Reconnective Healing frequency. I did not dwell on my form and worry about proper technique like many of the other students who were used to doing things differently. I didn't know any better. This was it for me: my first and only training. I just played with the energy. I was childlike and having fun with it. I was focused on feeling the sensations through my hands.

When we practiced on each other, we would watch the different "registers." Eric referred to these registers as physical or physiologic responses to connecting with the frequency such as eyelids flutter, the stomach may gurgle, the toes or fingers may move in a jerky fashion, just to name a few. These were the more common types of responses that we could sense as a connection to this new higher frequency being introduced. It was captivating, and it certainly kept our attention as the three sets of hands hovered and moved over the person lying on the table. My stomach would gurgle almost the entire time and make some weird noises. These things were validations that we were connecting with the energy. I would pay attention to how different areas of the body felt when I moved my hands. One area may feel cold; then I would move my hand to another spot on the body, and it may feel warmer. When my hands moved along the body, I felt a stronger connection in certain places; and as my hands moved along other areas, I could hardly feel anything.

This was what we did in our practice groups. It was easy to do and fun. Still, many people could not grasp it and were constantly asking questions about proper form and technique. "What do I do with my hands?" was repeated ad nauseam. As I have said before, people don't get simple. The most difficult concept for people to learn was just to play with the energy and let your awareness be with the person on the table. I considered it a blessing that I had not been trained in any other type of healing to draw experience from. I wasn't worried about making symbols with my hands and proper positioning over the body as other healers were trained to do using other frequencies.

I was in awe of this energy. I would go home at night and place the attention on my hands to "bring in the energy" just to make sure it was still there. I was a little surprised at first how the energy was always present. I wondered if it might just disappear once I went home. But sure enough, whenever I focused on my hands, the familiar tingling sensation would come right back. I could access the energy whenever I wanted, wherever I wanted. I would be out shopping or driving in my car or possibly watching television, and I would briefly place my attention on my hands to "activate" them just to make sure the energy was still there. *Was this all real?* This was my way of validating that it was.

The Practitioner's Expectation of the Outcome

If the healer you are working with does not believe in the work that they do, this will affect the outcome of the healing. I have met other healers, even Reconnective Healers, who say to me that they can't believe that this can work. A few of them were even in my training class with Eric. We were trained together. We were taught the same technique, worked with the same frequency, received the same information—so why were my healings "more powerful" as they described? My belief. I expected the healing to happen. I didn't just wave my hands around thinking, *This is not possible. I'm not really a healer. I can't believe this person is really expecting to be healed of this.*

I had a client who came to see me after recently having a session with another Reconnective Healer. He explained that during the energy healing he was very relaxed and enjoying the experience then, "All of a sudden the healer started belting out some high-pitched vocal notes!" Evidently, she felt that the energy could not possibly work alone, so she thought she would throw in some sound therapy, too, hoping that the frequency of her on key notes would produce a desirable result and adjust his vibration. He was caught so off-guard that he became very tense and uncomfortable for the remainder of the session.

This is a type of *healing potpourri* where you do not believe in what you are doing and throw a bunch of different modalities at the client hoping something will work. Our thoughts manifest as real energy. If the thought of the healer is, *This is not working. I know this can't work,* then this is what you will manifest—a poor outcome. Even though the healings come from a higher source, the healer should be a balanced vessel for the energy to flow through. *The consciousness of the healer can alter the energy being channeled.* These thoughts are real and manifest as physical vibrations that will negatively impact the work.

I know the Universe will provide the appropriate healing. I know this frequency is powerful. What do I do during a session? Enjoy myself. I remind myself before I start the session to remain in the present and let my awareness just be with the client. This may sound silly, but when we have sixty thousand random thoughts a day, I don't want to start thinking about my to-do-list or daydream about what I am having for lunch later. I am focused, present, and open to whatever happens.

In a session, I am not trying to direct the energy flow. I am in a state of being present and observing the sensations I am feeling. Actually, it is a very childlike state. I am in awe of all the different sensations I am experiencing. This helps to keep me present during the session.

When I first started to facilitate sessions, it was difficult for me not to focus on the end result. You want people to get the healing they want. You want them to be happy. There is some ego involved as well. You want to have the reputation as a *good healer*. I realized when I had an expectation of a miraculous result by the end of the session, I was anxious. Will their symptoms resolve? I was creating a performance anxiety. If the client still had symptoms after the session, I felt as if I had not been effective. It did not matter if they had the condition for decades and had spent thousands of dollars in medical bills over the years and were still suffering. Many clients who came to see me were there as a last resort for resolution of their condition, somewhat of a last-ditch effort on their part.

Energy Medicine is not about controlling; it is about allowing.

If I try to direct the healing and focus on the outcome, instead of just allowing the energy to flow through me, I am lowering the frequency I am working with. If I were to do this, I am controlling the energy, controlling the outcome. I trust in the higher intelligence from the source energy that the appropriate healing will take place at this time in the person's life in accordance with their higher self for their highest good.

One person may experience a dramatic result at the time the session is completed, and for another it could take weeks or longer. Some clients may never receive the physical healing that was hoped for but may have another resolution of a condition or issue, even if this resolution takes place on a spiritual or an emotional level. It does give me solace to know that there is a higher intelligence that is taking place, and the person will have the appropriate healing at the appropriate time in their life.

I realized not everything is evident at the time. If the healing they expected did not occur by the end of the session, the energy is still working with them and continuing to unfold. It could happen in a few days, maybe a few weeks or even longer.

What Is *Your* Expectation?

It is the *expectation* of the outcome that seems to be different with energy medicine as opposed to conventional therapy. When people go to the doctor, they expect medical tests and prescriptions for drugs and repeat follow up visits—sometimes for a lifetime. They expect to still have the disease, but have the disease with no symptoms.

Modern science has not even cured the common cold. Other than taking a course of antibiotics for an infection, there are very few things that are cured. People are given medications to treat the symptoms. Doctors don't say, "I will heal you. I will restore balance and harmony to the body."

Doctors say, "Here is your prescription." Most Americans are on at least three or four prescription drugs. We have become a pill-popping society. The expectation is to leave the office with a prescription. The placebo effect starts to go into effect as soon as the prescription is held in their hands.

Even the jargon is different. Doctors and patients use "cure." Healers use "balanced." I think the word healer seems to draw a connotation like in the movie *Faith Healer* with Steve Martin. It's a funny movie! He touches people on the head and says, "You're healed!!" and they fall backward and praise Jesus for the sudden healing of their affliction. In the movie, Steve Martin changes into this silver jacket, completely adorned with at least a hundred shiny little-mirrored pieces. Think of a walking disco ball. That's what he looks like!

He is running around the congregation yelling, "I feel a healing comin' on! Are you ready for a miracle?!" He touches people on the head as he passes each aisle in the tent of the makeshift church screaming a few "hallelujahs" as he is throwing a walker and a pair of crutches across the stage.

This is a whole production. People want the show. They want us to touch them and poof—the miracle! There seems to be an expectation with the word healer that portrays an image of touching someone and all their afflictions are gone in an instant. Maybe I should start throwing in a couple of "hallelujahs" during my sessions for an added effect. Doctors are healers too, but the expectation of a medical professional is to diagnose and prescribe a pill or perform a medical test for further diagnosis.

What Are You Preventing?

My sister recently scheduled a colonoscopy. As I drove her early in the morning to the office for her procedure, I asked, "Why are you having this done?"

"Because I am now at the age where this is what you are supposed to do," she replied naturally as if giving me helpful medical advice.

"This isn't preventative medicine," I said. "Preventative medicine is not going to the doctor and having tests done to make sure you don't have anything. You're just having a colonoscopy and finding out if it was normal or abnormal. What did your prevent?"

I couldn't seem to help myself as I continued with, "What did you prevent by paying for an expensive test? Preventative medicine is getting enough sleep, reducing stress, eating fresh, healthy foods, and drinking pure water, taking good quality vitamins and supplements like probiotics."

I finally paused and waited for her response. After a few moments of silence, I continued, "Do you take probiotics?" I asked her.

"What's a probiotic!" was her reply. I turned on the radio so we could relax for the rest of the drive and decided that after the procedure I was going to apologize to my sister for bringing this up right before her colonoscopy. I don't know why I started this conversation during the drive to her procedure. It was not the appropriate time to have this conversation. Okay, it's been established; I'm not perfect. With that being said, we do not have true preventative medicine in this country.

Having procedures done to see if something is wrong is not preventing an illness or condition. All these tests do is give you a yes or no answer. I am certainly not saying these tests do not have value and should not be done. I am only pointing out that many of these diagnostic procedures that are considered "preventative medicine" is not a prevention of what is already there.

These tests are diagnostic tools, not preventative measures.

Preventative medicine is being in tune with your body. When we have a problem, it starts out on an energetic level before it manifests into physical symptoms. The physical symptoms are a message to us that something is wrong and needs our attention. The issue that needs to be addressed is an energy imbalance. Correcting the energy imbalance is one form of preventative medicine, along with taking good care of yourself by eating healthy, exercising, drinking lots of good clean water, and reducing stress in your life. Acupuncture, chiropractic care, and other modalities also work on helping blocked energy to flow through the body.

There is no single treatment that is 100% effective for 100% of the people. This is why it is so important to have other options available to us. Most people with chronic illness have been seeing doctor after doctor for years trying to find relief from their symptoms. Many of them have taken multiple drugs, which have failed. After awhile, it becomes difficult to tell anymore whether the symptoms are from the illness or a side effect of all the combined drugs.

People are so used to taking medications to prevent symptoms that they may think of the pill as a cure. I have had physicians say to me how frustrating medicine has become because patients will say, "Just give me a pill."

Doctors will say, "You need to lose forty pounds; you have high cholesterol; you are pre-diabetic."

And patients will respond, "Great, doc . . . just give me a pill."

Most of us are not motivated to change the underlying condition to help restore the body into a more balanced state. "Just give me a pill" has become the new mantra as doctors' medical training consists of what pill to prescribe for each condition. It can be very frustrating for medical professionals as well when their patients go right back into old habits after events like a heart attack or complications from diabetes without making lifestyle changes and solely depend on taking a pill.

Wait a minute . . . the doctor just came into the recovery area where I am waiting with my sister, "Your colon is textbook! Completely normal. No polyps. No inflammation. Everything looks great!"

"I guess I'm good then for another ten years!" I blurted out, and the doctor laughed.

CHAPTER 5

We Are Not a Machine

We see things not as they are, but as we are.

—*H.M. Tomlinson*

Modern medicine as we know it today views the body as a machine with replaceable parts. Many medical doctors do not think the mind or emotions have anything to do with our health. We are taught to believe that our body just functions automatically. Each separate part of our body knows what to do as if we have no input at all. This is because we live in a country where medical doctors treat us like "Frankenstein," compiled of body parts that need to be treated separately. We have brain doctors, heart doctors, lung doctors, bone doctors, digestive tract doctors, skin doctors, etc.

When we take an anatomy and physiology class, we learn about the structure of our body, the structure of bones, the organs, and their function. Unfortunately, we do not learn that our thoughts and our attitudes have an effect on our overall health. We are in constant communication with the cells in our body. Our cells respond to our thoughts. Our cells respond to our emotions. Our cells respond to our voice. We are in control. We act as though we are in a game of Ping-Pong, and we are the ball being forced in one direction after another with no control whatsoever. *We treat our bodies like a plant. Keep it fed and watered, and it will live and grow.* That's it.

What a Lunatic!

Several years ago, I had a lunch with a doctor's office with three neurologists in the group. Drug reps schedule lunches with doctors' offices so that we can have more time with the doctors to discuss our products as opposed to a quick stand up detail for thirty seconds between patients. One of the doctors who came into the lunch sat down to eat and was shaking his head mumbling, "What a lunatic!"

"What?! Who's a lunatic?" I asked to clarify. I just wanted to make certain he wasn't referring to me. Maybe he didn't like the chicken I brought.

"My patient!" he replied. "I have had this cold for three months," he explained. "One of my patients brought me a book—mind over body. What a nut! Can you believe it? He said I could heal my body with my mind. He's nuts!!"

"Do you believe the mind has anything to do with how our body responds?" I asked, fishing for an expert opinion after his little rant.

"OF COURSE NOT!" he exclaimed, as if I was joining the lunatic club.

"So you don't think our emotions have anything to do with disease and illness?"

"Absolutely not!" He said, shaking his head and a little miffed that I would ask such a ridiculous question.

As I sat there, I wanted to ask, "Well, doctor . . . then how would you explain the placebo effect?" I didn't ask. I decided this was not the agenda of my visit with him today. My job was to educate him about the drug I am selling for the pharmaceutical company, not trying to educate him on the mind-body connection. Apparently, he is a neurologist who seems to think the mind comes separate from the body. On second thought, there may be some truth to this. Lately, I have many days where I would swear to you that I left my mind at home whenever I went out.

There are many books that deal with the mind-body connection for illness and disease. Dr. Bernie Siegel wrote several books about his experience with cancer patients and their emotional state affecting their outcome. If the mind-body connection is not real, then how can the many documented cases of spontaneous remission be explained when Dr. Siegel's cancer patients changed not only their lifestyle but their attitude and emotions toward their illness. They healed! *They healed themselves!*

I have to say, though, I sat there utterly stunned. This comment was from a neurologist who deals with the brain. Certainly he would understand that our emotions, whether negative or positive, affect our well-being. Does he not think that stress can cause physical illness? I already know the answer. Oh well, he seemed to be enjoying the chicken.

The truth is, our body is a functioning energy system, not a machine of separate parts. The energy needs to flow throughout the body for us to maintain a healthy state of being. Our thoughts, emotions, beliefs, as well as stress, all influence how our energy flows. If our energy is blocked, we have illness and disease.

Why Is Our Energy Blocked?

Chronic emotional stress is one of the main causes of physical illness. Our emotions—positive and negative—affect our emotional health, which in turn affect the flow of energy through our meridian system and our chakras.

If you want to know how your energy is flowing, take a look at your emotions. If your emotional state is predominantly hatred, anger, resentment, jealousy, greed, and other negative emotions, you will have an energy flow imbalance that will impact the organs in the body. If your emotions are positive, and hopefully your default emotions are that of love, joy, happiness, optimism, and gratitude, this is the information the cells in your body are responding to.

We have many different forms of stress on the body from internal factors and external stress from our daily life. Internal stress is how we *react* to life and the hurdles and obstacles thrown at us daily. How do we deal with the relationships with the people in our lives? We each handle life circumstances in a different way. *What could cause one person to totally "lose it" and have a full-blown anxiety attack may not even faze another person.*

External stress could come from our jobs, paying the bills, taking care of the kids, and maintaining our homes, cars, yards, etc. The economy has been uncertain, and many people in the workforce no longer have job security. More and more people find themselves out of work, and the unstable economy has made it difficult to find employment. The pace of the world is moving faster and faster. It seems to be more difficult just to keep up with our lives. Healthcare coverage is another stressful factor we all have to contend with in this country. If we get sick, will we be able to afford treatment for loved ones and ourselves?

This chronic stress not only depletes our energy but also causes fatigue, depression, anxiety, a generalized lack of motivation, and malaise. Our body responds to these stress signals and releases chemicals that perpetuate this imbalance even further. Our chakras, which are like energy vortexes, become blocked. The energy that flows through them becomes impeded, affecting every organ of the body. If our energy is blocked and imbalanced, we become imbalanced. This imbalance leads to illness.

It's All in Your Head

A physician may say to their patient, "Your illness is psychosomatic," when they cannot determine the cause of the physical symptoms. "It's all in your head," a patient may hear during an office visit. Doctors have believed for many years, and some still believe, that fibromyalgia, which mainly affects women, is psychosomatic. They thought the women were all crazy! Having physical symptoms of joint pain and fatigue with no underlying cause? The doctors were actually right.

All illness and disease have an underlying component of being psychosomatic.

We cannot separate our mind from our body. Our mind is always involved. Always. Psychosomatic means that there is a *mental* and *emotional* aspect of our symptoms. Our mind influences our body around the clock. This is why we get sick during times of continual stress. When we are anxious, depressed, run down, we get sick. Our constant internal dialogue is giving our body messages that we respond to. Even how quickly we heal is due to a psychosomatic effect.

There is always a mental and emotional aspect of our physical symptoms, even if we have the common cold.

Remember when doctors told patients that stress caused ulcers? It seems like an oxymoron how some doctors still say the mind does not have anything to do with illness, and yet since they did not know what caused an ulcer—this was linked to stress? If these doctors don't "buy into" the mind-body connection then why was stress (emotional state) linked to ulcers?

People will get a headache when they are stressed. Why? Because all things are psychosomatic. Again, our mental and emotional state always affects the health of our body 24/7. I'll say it again: everything is psychosomatic because we cannot remove our mind from our body. This does not mean that we do not experience physical symptoms. These physical symptoms are real. No matter what the cause of fibromyalgia is, these women are experiencing physical symptoms and suffering.

What does psychosomatic really mean? Psychosomatic means that the mind and body are both involved. Our mind and body are connected and involved in everything. Some doctors have used the term for stating that the patients illness is imaginary. If they can't find the cause, they determine there is no justifiable, real physical symptom. Unless you believe that the mind is always running a separate program that does not interfere with and not integrated in the body, you will see that all healing and illness has an underlying psychosomatic component.

Our mind influences our body in every illness.

The Most Powerful Medicine Is the Emotional State of the Mind

As mentioned at the beginning of this chapter, even the placebo effect supports this mind-body connection. The word placebo comes from the Latin word "placer" meaning "I shall please." A placebo is a harmless substance used to help create the expectation to the patient that it will have a benefit. The placebo could be a sugar pill or another inactive formulation of the actual drug to "fake out" the patient that they are taking the real thing. Basically, the placebo is a "fake drug." It is usually used as a control in a clinical study to determine if the "real drug," hoping to gain approval from the FDA, actually works.

All treatments and medicines have a placebo effect. Even the African witch doctors' treatments have a placebo effect. The placebo effect has been proven in numerous clinical studies and has been reported in medical journals. The placebo effect is around a 30% response rate. Just think, if there is a clinical trial from a drug company and 30% of the patients had a response to the drug that could be due to the placebo effect. Usually, one arm of the study is the placebo (sugar pill) versus the actual drug, which needs to show a higher response rate than the placebo arm for approval from the FDA.

The prescription drugs you take have a placebo effect as well. This effect could be influenced by your doctor. For example, let's say your doctor sends you home with a sample of the medication you will be taking and says, "I am confident this drug will work for you. I have had great success with it! All my patients loved it and experienced no side effects." Already the placebo effect has kicked in before you leave the office. It is this expectation of having a positive outcome that will affect your result.

There is also a Latin word "nocebo," which means "I shall harm." Here is another example of an expectation of the outcome. Let's say that another doctor gives the same sample of the medication to one of his patients and says, "This drug may not work for you. I don't have a lot of confidence in this medication. A few of my patients had some severe side effects." This is an example of the nocebo effect. The nocebo effect is the expectation of a negative or harmful outcome. In both instances, the patient has already created an emotional attachment to what they will experience.

The placebo/nocebo effect is validation that the mind-body connection does exist!

Is energy healing due to the placebo effect? One could argue that energy medicine results are only a placebo effect. As with the medications, every healing technique also has a placebo effect because our emotions toward everything always affect the outcome to some degree. If the outcome is only due to a placebo effect, then how can it be explained that animals respond to energy medicine. Animals also respond to acupuncture and chiropractic treatments as well. The animals are not thinking, "Oh good! Melissa is here doing a healing session on me. I expect to have a favorable outcome."

Body Speak

Our mind and our body are integrated as ONE. You can think of our mind as the software running the program for our body. When we have *symptoms*, this is *body speak*. Our body is speaking to us, alerting us that we are out of balance. Pay Attention! What happens when someone is speaking to you and you don't listen? They speak LOUDER. Your body will do the same thing in the form of more symptoms until you listen.

There have been numerous reports of miraculous healings occurring when people have made lifestyle changes and/or belief changes and their illness disappeared. Why? Because the program that was running changed, and the body now responds to the new information received.

We are constantly running a *mind story* that is playing the same theme until we acknowledge something isn't working in our life and rewrite it. When you change your mind story, your body is running a new software program. How can you do this? By changing "the what" in your life that isn't working. Guess what?! Your body responds and can do so very quickly for a spontaneous remission of illness and disease.

CHAPTER 6

Who Will Benefit?

Build your own dreams, or someone else will hire you to build theirs.
—Farrah Gray

Most people always ask, "Have you treated anyone else who has had XYZ? Well . . . how was the outcome? Were they healed?" I don't consider it relevant to discuss another client's outcome for a particular condition. Just because one person experienced a success with a particular ailment is not commensurate with another person's healing. The healing that a person receives was the *appropriate healing for that person* at that time in their life. People have their own life experience and unique individualized lesson plan. Just because one person was healed of arthritis or a torn ligament, broken finger, or even cancer, does not in any way mean that another person will have a similar outcome.

Think of it this way: **Same disease—same symptoms—does not equal same outcome.**

This statement is not just true for energy healing. This statement is true for *any* healing, whether it is conventional medicine or alternative therapies. This is why there are no guarantees in medicine. The person will have the appropriate healing and experience he/she was meant to have.

In addition to the physical imbalance, there are spiritual and emotional issues in the mind and body that manifest as physical symptoms that are different for each individual; therefore, the solution is different for each individual. *All healing is done from within.* Possibly, we needed this life circumstance for us to awaken and realize the way we were living our life was negatively impacting our well-being. The illness could be the catalyst for a major life change. When we are in balance on a physical, emotional, and spiritual level, we heal.

The way to achieve this balance is *not standardized*. It is *individualized*.

This is energy with a spiritual component with intelligence. *It is my higher self working with your higher self with the intelligence of God.* I am not directing the energy for a certain outcome. I am channeling the energy and allowing the experience to present itself in the appropriate way for all concerned.

Does Everyone Benefit?

I believe that everyone has a benefit from an energy healing session. There are many reasons why a person may not get the healing that they hope for when they come in for a session. It could be their own receptivity to the healing. Maybe they are not ready to accept the energy and move forward with their healing. This may sound harsh, but some people are not ready to heal. There are people who have become accustomed to the role of playing the victim. Their life revolves around their illness: the medical treatments, the doctors' appointments, the medications, even their relationships are more focused on support and caregiving. It has become a part of who they are and how they relate to the world. Without the illness, they may feel as though their identity is lost.

Becoming healthy again would require a shift in consciousness and a major life change they may not be ready for. Their illness could be their security blanket. Without this "crutch" in life, the comfortable and known way of living and relating to their world could transform to the unknown and possibly uncomfortable new way of being and living. *The conscious mind may want to move forward with the healing, but the subconscious mind may have another agenda because the soul is not ready at this particular time to move forward.*

It may not be time for the person on a soul level to move forward with their expected healing at this particular time in their life. Maybe the lesson has not yet been learned. Some of us choose pre-incarnation to experience an illness for our growth and learning. We plan our lifetime of what we want to experience and learn just as we plan the day and time of our birth in accordance with our life plan and lesson. Let's say that in this lifetime we want to evolve from point A to point R. Without having an illness to propel us forward in our evolution, we might only go from point A to point G.

When we have an illness, we are forced to internalize things. When we do this, we process information in a new way. We look for answers. The difference is: *we look within for answers.* This is especially true when we are faced with a life-threatening illness. This is when people tend to incorporate God into their lives. Oftentimes, it is not until tragedy strikes that we look for a connection to a higher source.

Why Don't People Heal?

We can't see the big picture. We cannot fully understand the magnitude of an illness. Poor health can show us things about ourselves that we need to change. Illness is not always a bad thing.

Oftentimes an illness is the catalyst for a great transformation taking place within us that will manifest into a life change.

We may experience a malady due to a life lesson we need to experience at a particular period during our lifetime. The ailment or condition may be occurring at this time because the person is going through a transformation on a soul level. Possibly this failing health could be forcing a person to look within themselves to create a huge shift in awareness and spiritual growth. Or maybe the person is off track of what they set out to accomplish in this lifetime, and this is the impetus compelling a life-altering change: ending a relationship that is not working, causing a job/career change, or relocating.

How we learn and evolve is by overcoming obstacles. If you have kids, especially teenagers, you know that if you do not let them have their own experience and make mistakes, they resent you because they want to understand fully and learn about life. This comes from their *own* experience of life, not someone else sharing with them about their past experience.

We certainly don't need a life or want a life where we have one obstacle and hardship after another, but we do need to learn lessons. It is no different than our kids in school. If the agenda were parties, entertainment, and playtime every day, what would they learn? They need some pre-planned lessons thrown in there during some of the fun in order to learn and grow to reach their fullest potential.

That is what our chart is. We plan an agenda of what we want to accomplish during our lifetime on Earth. It's as if we wrote our own play and when we are born we are the actor on the *"stage of life."* You can think of this planet as one huge stage with seven billion actors playing out their roles. We throw certain lessons in there to work on in order to create many different experiences. At times, we are the teacher, and other times we are the student. There are situations created where we keep experiencing the same lesson over and over until we learn from it and move on to another lesson. Just like a typical school. This is why I refer to our incarnation on Earth: "The School of Life." You can read this chapter in my book, *It's Just MY Nonsense.*

What would we learn in life if everything were always perfect! We create obstacles and challenges in life to learn more about who we are. Think of our life experience as part of our *unveiling.* We are in a process of learning who we really are.

We are gradually lifting the veil as we overcome each hurdle in life to reveal who we are on a soul level.

At the time, we can't see this experience from another perspective, but once the experience is over we have greater clarity to view what we went through from a higher perspective. When I say a higher perspective, I am referring to a new vantage point, more of a bird's eye view to see a bigger picture of an event or circumstance that has happened. It's as if we now become an observer of the experience. At this time, the spiritual reason may be clearer.

We are in school all the time. We don't see the building or hear the bell ring for the start of class. We don't need to. The class begins here on Earth when we are born, and the class is over when we die and go home.

Ughhh!! Go Away Guilters!

I have met people, who profess to be very spiritual, yet who will guilt you at every opportunity. (I'm sure you met them, too!) These people seem to believe that every bad thing and every illness we have we brought upon ourselves. *"It's your own fault. Stop doing this to yourself!"* they may be overheard saying when what we need in our life is for our friends and family to be loving and compassionate. There are times when something like this is appropriate. For instance, when we are hanging on to negative feelings like revenge, hatred, and still dealing with unresolved anger and forgiveness issues that are destroying our health, a comment like this may be a good wake-up call.

Is there someone in your life that you need to forgive? Hanging on to negative emotions, conflicts, and past hurts can wreak havoc on our bodies and spiritual well-being. We not only become energetically drained and lethargic, but our immune system becomes lowered, and we get sick easier. These negative emotions create energy blockages that keep us from health and vitality.

There is no reason for anyone to place judgment on another person about why they are sick or have an obstacle to overcome. These *spiritual guilters* bestow guilt at every opportunity. These people will shame you into thinking that you are culpable for everything and cause pain to your loved ones and yourself by your inadequate ability to maintain perfection in your life and health at all times.

You are shamed into believing that everything is entirely your fault, with well-deserved suffering for your lack of *spiritual finesse*. You now feel worse than ever! My advice to you: avoid these guilters.

The guilters are guilty of judgment.

These people do not know your life plan and lessons you are learning. The truth is: everyone learns at their own desire and their own pace.

What Goes on During a Session?

A healing session is unique and individualized. No two people will have the exact same experience. *Each person will interact with the energy in a different way.* There are tangibles that we may see such as a bone heal, or a skin lesion or wound become better. There are also intangibles that we may not see after a session: a person's vibration increasing, energy blockages being removed, anxiety and depression being relieved, stress reduction and immune function being enhanced, and so forth.

At times, information may be given to the client that will help assist with moving forward in their healing. This information could be in the form of messages from angels or guides. A memory that had been buried in the subconscious mind and long forgotten may surface to the consciousness to be healed. These are the reasons why I believe everyone does benefit from a healing session, even if the expected outcome is not received immediately.

After the session has ended, the energy continues working with the person. *The energy is still there harmonizing with the individual.* The energy does not stop working just because the healing session is over. The end result is not always evident immediately after the session. Usually, improvements continue to unfold over time.

For a person to have a disease is an unnatural and unbalanced state of being. If someone is spiritually and mentally healthy but has a physical ailment, they are unbalanced. Just as a person who appears to be fine physically, but mentally/emotionally they are unbalanced. All three need to be in balance for a person to be in true harmony. Energy Medicine works to assist in restoring balance and harmony physically, emotionally, and spiritually.

Even if the client does not have the result they were hoping for, there is certainly work that is being done for them. In most instances, I do one session. If the individual does not have the outcome that was hoped for, it may be best to wait until another time. This does not mean that you should not have another healing session at a later date. This is generally why I do not do more than two to three healing sessions for a person.

Maybe there is another healing modality or another medical option that will better suit them as well. There are some maladies that may last a lifetime. When we planned our chart before the incarnation, sometimes we do put an illness or deformity for the growth of the soul and/or the growth of the soul group of others who have incarnated together to learn a similar lesson.

There are people that, on a subconscious level, may be blocking their own healing. The conscious mind is ready to move forward and heal, but the higher self knows there is another agenda going on and the healing is blocked at this time.

Even if the desired outcome of the session does not happen, the cells are responding to the frequency. There is always work that is being done and a benefit. We think of healing as a cure on a physical level, but there is an emotional and spiritual healing taking place as well. We can't always see what is going on. We can't see chakras vibrating faster and meridians opening to allow a greater flow of energy. We can't see a person's vibration being raised. We can't see the spiritual awakening. We can't see karma being balanced. Even if most people cannot actually see these things taking place, these things can be *perceived*.

On a soul level, we become stronger when we go through experiences and overcome them. An illness may be what is needed to force us to slow down our life and see what is not working for us. With this new awareness, we will now be able to understand what life changes are appropriate so that we can have a life of better health and less stress.

We Are Infinite Beings

People have argued whether the human being is eternal. When we die, do we cease to exist? We know that our body decays after we die. We are mourned and buried. But our essence is pure energy. Energy can be altered. Energy cannot be destroyed. Does this mean our energy lives forever?

Theresa Caputo, also known as the *Long Island Medium* channels spirits from the other side. Why is she able to talk to the dead? First of all, she is a very gifted medium who can see and talk to those souls who have departed. Even more important, she is able to talk to people who have crossed over because their energy is not destroyed. The energy of the person who incarnated upon this planet still exists in a higher vibration. When we are in our human bodies on Earth, we are in a very dense form, which vibrates at a lower frequency than back home. When we die and leave this earthly existence, we are *Light Beings,* meaning we are vibrating at a much higher frequency and emitting more light.

Theresa Caputo's work, for many people, has validated the truth that *we are Energy.* Theresa turned many disbelievers to believers that there is life "on the other side." People, who in the past may have thought that communicating with departed souls was a hoax, are now on her wait list to talk to their deceased loved ones. Communication with those souls who have crossed over is a validation that our energy is not destroyed. Our energy is altered from a lower to a higher vibrational existence. We experience a *transformation of our energy* from denser to lighter state. You can also think of this transformation from lower to higher vibration. More important: *We are Infinite Beings.*

During our incarnation, we are spiritual beings who are pretending to be human. When we leave this realm, we leave the density of our human bodies behind. We are much less dense than we were during our existence on Earth. When we are less dense, we vibrate at a higher frequency. Light beings vibrate higher. Human beings vibrate at a lower frequency.

The *human beings* who have crossed over now vibrate at a much higher frequency: *light beings.* This is why their higher vibration is not visible to us in this lower dimensional existence that we occupy on this planet. Even when our deceased loved ones come around to visit and comfort us, we can't see them. We may sense their presence and feel their energy around us, though.

When we are "back home," with our lightness of being, we have *enlightenment.* This is why you can think of enlightenment as en**light**enment. We are able to see more of the big picture of our life as our consciousness and our awareness is far greater and greatly expanded than when we were here on Earth.

When we leave our physical body and return home, we have more light and are awakened. We are no longer playing the game of being human in this higher realm. We are purely spiritual beings once again.

CHAPTER 7

Can We Change Our DNA?

If you want to find the secrets of the universe, think in terms
of energy, frequency and vibration.

—Nicola Tesla

Does Energy Change Our DNA?

Do you realize that during an energy healing session your DNA is being altered? The healing occurs at the cellular level. Your DNA can actually be improved with using the energy to heal. What happens during an energy healing session? The energy is changed. *The vibration of your DNA is changed.*

Actually, our DNA is being changed in every moment of our existence. The frequencies on the planet, the foods we eat, our thoughts, emotions, even our beliefs, all affect and alter our cellular structure. Energy Medicine just speeds up the process and introduces a frequency with the intention to provide balance and harmony to the body. The distinction of an Energy Medicine Healing session is the intention for healing and restoring balance.

Every cell at the DNA level becomes entrained to the new frequency being introduced. When a higher vibration is introduced to a lower vibration, the lower vibration now becomes elevated and vibrates faster. This is what happens to our cellular structure. Every cell, organ, system, and structure of our body is changed. Elevated to a higher vibration. Elevated to a higher frequency. This is why the higher vibration energy is very healing.

Can Focused Intention Change DNA?

Researchers at the Institute of HeartMath in Boulder Creek, CA, studied the effect of focused intention to change DNA. The article "Modulation of DNA Conformation by Heart-Focused Intention" supported evidence of the effect of positive emotion and focused intention to alter DNA in vitro (test tube).[4]

The ten participants in the study focused their feelings on love and appreciation while also focusing their *intention* to either wind or unwind the sample of DNA in the test tube. This resulted in a significant change in the DNA sample. An interesting aspect of this study showed that both heart-based emotion (love and appreciation) *and* intention needed to be present to create a change in DNA. If the intention was there without the positive emotion, there was no change. If the heart-based emotion was present, but the participant did not have an intended focus to change the DNA, the sample had no significant change.

The researchers also tested whether the participant could affect the DNA sample from a distance. They referred to these studies as nonlocal experiments. In these experiments, the participant was located 0.5 miles away from the DNA sample. Again, a significant change in the DNA occurred, even at such a large distance. The participant wasn't just in another room in the same building while trying to affect the DNA sample to either wind or unwind; the person was a half-mile away! Just as in the previous (local) experiment, both the *heart-based positive emotion* and *intention* needed to be present to alter the DNA.

The important aspect of this study shows that DNA *does* respond to our intentions and emotions. We now have documented evidence that we can intentionally change our DNA and it can be altered. This is no longer just a theory. The change in our DNA occurs at the cellular level. If we are changing DNA, we are creating a change in our cellular structure.

Although the DNA used in the study was from an outside source and placed in a test tube, the authors state, "While the DNA utilized in this experiment was derived from an exogenous source, it is likely that an individual's own DNA would be more 'tuned' or resonant, and therefore even more responsive, to that person's intentions."[5] It is possible that our intentions would magnify the changes in our own DNA, far greater than the alterations that were seen with using the test tube DNA.

The results shown in this study bring up an interesting question: If we can change our DNA with positive emotions (love, gratitude, appreciation, compassion) with the required intention to physically change our DNA, what effect do negative emotions have?

Do Negative Emotions Change Our DNA?

Although this study was not designed to test how negative emotions alter our DNA, there was one study participant who was frustrated and upset. He was not able to focus his intention to change the DNA. He did agree to at least hold the DNA sample to be studied. When the DNA sample he was holding was studied, it revealed that his energy produced an increased winding in the DNA. It was also determined that the physical/chemical structure in one or more of the bases was altered.

The reviewed data from the one participant who was angry and frustrated demonstrated a winding (*tightening*) of the DNA without creating any intention to do so. It's as if his negative emotions was working on the DNA by default: the DNA was reacting to his energy adversely, even without any conscious intention on his part to do so. Also evident was the abnormal alteration in the structure of the base molecules of the DNA.

If we can see these abnormalities from negative emotions in the DNA test tube samples, just consider the magnitude of the damage we can do to our own DNA with repetitive stress and negative emotional states of anger, hatred, jealousy, and revenge. As we had seen in the study, even with the absence of intention to alter the DNA, the emotional energy of these negative thoughts and feelings are destructive to our cells. Have you ever heard the expression when you are angry, *"Don't get so wound up!"*?

This is what happened to the DNA sample with negative emotions in the study from the one participant only holding the DNA sample. When the DNA starts to wind, the DNA is tighter. What happens when the DNA is wound tighter and tighter? *The DNA is shortened.*

This is essentially what our cells are doing. They are winding and tightening, causing stress and damage. Just think what happens when our DNA is shortened. Our life force is shortened as well. When our cells are sick—we are sick!

Our cells respond to *all* our thoughts and emotions on a conscious level, even our subconscious thoughts, emotions, and feelings that have been buried and suppressed on an unconscious level. There are times when these repressed emotions that have been buried, possibly since childhood, have spontaneously surfaced during a hypnotic session, or possibly during or following a traumatic event. *Our cells still respond to these repressed emotions even if we do not remember them on a conscious level.*

When we are happy and joyful, feel gratitude, and bring laughter into our lives, we become "unwound." This is why I refer to these emotions as lighter emotions. Not only are these emotions associated with a higher vibration and corresponding higher frequency, but they also cause our tight DNA to relax and unwind. Doesn't it now make sense how adversely stress destroys our bodies and shortens our life?

There Is No Fooling Our Cells

Frequency continually and constantly influences and changes our DNA. This is ALL frequency. Frequency from the Earth, electronic devices, cell phones, and even our power lines transform our DNA. Sounds can also affect and alter our DNA. This is how sound healing works.

Some frequencies heal; some frequencies harm.

Everything that alters our cells also alters our DNA, since this is the building block of our cellular structure. The DNA, contained in the cell's nucleus, is the command center of the cell. The nucleus controls the cell much like our brain controls the body. You can think of the nucleus as the brain regulating the activities of each cell. As a side note, red blood cells do not have a nucleus and do not have DNA. This is why they have such a short lifespan of about 4 months. Without DNA they do not replicate.

If energy alters the DNA, it is possible to re-program our DNA to fight disease and cure illness. I believe the future of healing will focus on frequency devices and Energy Medicine Healers as a non-invasive modality without the need for painful surgery and other diagnostic procedures.

Our emotions and intentions change our DNA. Most people are familiar with using affirmations to change our habitual negative thoughts and mind chatter into positive thoughts. Affirmations are used to change how we think. Anything we do with repetition can become a habit for us. Our negative thoughts and negative daily mind chatter can easily become our default way of thinking. We can break this habit with practice and intention to do so.

Positive affirmations help us to break this negative cycle and create a more positive way of thinking. These higher vibration thoughts and feelings emit a higher light frequency that alters our cells. This is why it is so important to be aware of our recurring thoughts and emotions.

Our cells are listening!

Since our cells are listening, it only makes sense that even with an intention to change our DNA we still need the heart-based positive emotions (love, gratitude, joy, laughter). For instance, let's say we intend for healing to take place within our cells, but we are angry and irritated by something that happened. Our body is tense, we feel stressed, and our cells are listening and responding to these messages. We are able to positively impact DNA with a focused intention to do so when this intention is coupled with positive emotions. Our DNA is changed in a negative way with stress and anger, and other negative emotions with *no intention* to do so. This is a significant difference.

If you expect the affirmations you are using to be effective, then say them with emotion and feeling. If the emotion is absent when you speak them, they are just words being said aloud. Remember, for a positive change to occur at the DNA level, we need to have the positive emotions along with the intention for change to happen. *There is no fooling our cells!*

CHAPTER 8

The Energy Is the Medicine

Energy Medicine is about changing our perception of what we think is possible to what we know is a possibility.

—Melissa Mintz

I Still Don't Get It?

I could be on the phone with a client for forty-five minutes and at the end of the conversation, I would hear, "I still don't get what you do." This is one of the reasons why I decided to write this book. Since I hear many of the same questions over and over, I thought, *Wouldn't it be nice, if I could reply, "An explanation to that question is in chapter 3 on page 49."* Clients seem to be confused about where the energy comes from and how it can assist them in their healing. I try to keep my reply simple; "I am bombarding you with energy. This energy helps to restore balance to the body."

"I still don't get how energy can heal?"

I continue to explain. "Think of it this way," I start out saying. "The *energy* is the *medicine*. I am transferring a higher vibration of energy to you. Every cell in your body will attune to this new energy to kick-start your body's own innate healing ability."

The silence tells me the prospective client is still confused and not even sure what follow up question to ask as they are still trying to process *energy is medicine*. "You can think of an Energy Medicine Healer as an energy catalyst," I add. "The energy is the catalyst that helps to rebalance the abnormal vibrations of the body to help you heal."

I have to admit; I am a little baffled as to why it is so important to understand as a step-by-step mechanism of how energy heals. First of all, healing with energy has a spiritual component as well. God, Energy, Source, Light, Love—whatever word you prefer to use to describe the energy—play a role in determining the appropriate outcome for the best interest of the person receiving the healing at this time in their life. When we pray, we don't say, "I have to fully understand God. First, prove to me there really is a God. Second, explain how prayer works. Third, prove to me that prayer will work. Also, I would like a guarantee that it *will* work."

In addition, the majority of us have all been patients before and seen medical doctors. When a doctor hands us a prescription for a drug do we say, "Doctor . . . I am not taking this until you fully explain to me how this drug works. I need to completely understand the mechanism of action before I swallow this medicine"?

Your doctor will look at you like you are crazy! First of all, your doctor does not know how every drug works. The researchers and scientists do not even know how most of these drugs work when they are discovered. The prescribing information for many approved drugs states "unknown mechanism of action."

It is not about understanding how they work. It is an acceptance that they do work.

When you have a medical test such as an MRI or a CAT scan, do you ask the technician, "How does this work"? Some people do. They want to know, mostly out of curiosity. The technician will give you a basic explanation. If you don't fully understand how the machine works, will you cancel the test?

I am certainly not saying we should not try to understand how things work and make informed decisions. Quite the contrary. I think that we should research things to better understand how to make safe and informed choices. Not everything can be fully explained and comprehended, but *we see that they work and accept that they work.*

How many of us know exactly how our cars work? We depend on them to get us where we want to go. When I am driving my car around I never think, *I wonder how this thing works.* I just drive. Almost everyone has a computer. When I write this book on my computer, I really don't care to know all the mechanics of how it works. I see that it does work.

When we relax in the evenings and watch our televisions, do we have to know completely how everything works to enjoy the show? Of course not, we know that it works. We enjoy the show. We appreciate the benefit of having and using all of these things. If I don't fully understand the mechanics of everything, it does not diminish the effectiveness. I know that it works. I see it working.

It's okay to accept that you may never have a full understanding of how energy can heal. If you think about it, it would be like saying, "I can fully understand God," since we are using source energy to heal.

Energy Medicine is a pain-free and non-invasive form of healing.

The most important thing: Be open to the experience. Allow the healing to come through that was meant for you.

Healing with Frequency

Energy Medicine to heal using frequency is not as "out there" as people think. Frequency in healing is not something new and not inherent to only alternative therapy techniques. Frequency is used today in mainstream medicine. Bone growth stimulators have been used successfully on broken bones that haven't fully healed after several months. This low-frequency electrical current stimulates the bone and the blood vessels around the broken bone to heal.

Frequency therapy has also been used to alleviate pain using sound waves from ultrasound or devices that generate an electromagnetic current to reduce pain and inflammation. We know that our heart works by a using electrical energy. A medical pacemaker is a device surgically implanted to help the heart beat in a regular rhythm that would mimic your normal heart function. Frequency and vibration *are* used as a treatment protocol in modern medicine; we just don't realize it. I would venture to say that your doctors don't realize this as well. We don't think of these devices as *energy medicine machines*, but in all the examples described above, the *energy* is the treatment.

Still, this is a difficult concept for most people to relate to. Healing with energy as the medicine is not taught in medical school. The doctors don't say to their patients, "Why don't you try an energy medicine session." They are doing what they have been trained to do—treating the patient with the tools they have available, which are usually drugs and surgery.

Healing with Energy

Now that you are more fully aware of how everything in the Universe is energy, doesn't it make sense that we can use this Universal Energy to heal? After all, as we now know, *we are energy*. We are the energy of our Creator, Source, Love, Light, whatever term you feel more comfortable with using. If we are of the same energy as our Creator, we are also *infinite beings*. This energy does not die. We move from our current existence of lower vibration (denser or *heavier*) to higher vibration (less dense or *lighter*) when we leave this earthly existence and cross over back home.

Just because energy is invisible, does not mean we cannot sense and feel the energy around us. The air around us is invisible. We don't focus on how we can breathe in the air. We don't say, "I still don't get where air is from?" We know that we breathe in the oxygen in the air, and we accept this as truth. Even though we can't see the air, we can see the pollutants in the air such as smoke and smog. We can feel the air by the wind blowing when it's breezy outside on a blustery day.

We can feel the energy, too. There are many ways to play with this energy and use it to self-heal and to heal others. Healing with energy is easy and natural. There is no need for me to devote an entire book on how to connect with energy or how to heal yourself and send healing energy to others. Using this life force energy to heal has always been available to human beings. We are energy. We recognize this energy. We remember this energy in every part of our being. Every cell responds to the new higher vibration introduced during an energy healing session.

So, what better way to heal (We are energy!) than by using energy? It sounds simple enough. It is our logical mind trying to overanalyze and complicate something simple because we are used to treating illness, disease, and deformities by providing drugs, surgery, and other various procedures. This has been our way of life. Healing with energy was the way healing was done in the beginning of our existence. We were aware of how vibration affected us and used this knowledge to heal. Singing, chanting, and drumming were also used to create a vibrational shift within us. In the future, healing with *energy as the medicine* will be a way of life and more readily accepted.

Time to play

Let's play! There are many ways to feel the energy. Have you ever rubbed your hands together briskly on a cold day trying to warm them up? I am doing this right now, so I can explain to you what I am feeling in my hands. Take a moment and do this along with me. Briskly rub the palms of your hands together either back and forth or in a circular motion for a few seconds. Can you feel your hands getting warm? When you stop rubbing your palms and bring your hands apart, do you feel the heat? Do your hands tingle? You may even feel a pulsing sensation. Now, slowly bring the palms of your hands toward each other just a few inches apart as if a rubber band is pulling them together. Now, slowly move your palms away from each other as if stretching the rubber band.

Place your attention and awareness on the feeling and sensations in the space between the palms of your hands as your move them together and then slowly apart. Focus on feeling the energy in the space between your palms as this energy constricts when you move your palms toward each other. When you slowly move your hands away from each other, place your attention on the space between your hands and feel the energy expand. Move your palms toward and then away from each other creating about a twelve-inch space between your palms to really start to feel the energy compress and expand. You are now consciously playing with energy.

Energy Slinky

Here is another example of how to connect with the energy. Remember playing with a slinky as a kid? The helical spring toy made of metal or plastic could stretch out and recoil to a flat stack of springs. You could place it on top of a flight of steps and watch it "walk down the steps," end over end until it reached the bottom of the staircase. In the 1960s and '70s, every kid I knew had one. We would place one end of the spiral coils on each palm and move our hands up and down to watch the wave of metal springs expand then reset.

Let's practice playing with the energy again. Take your arms, bent at the elbow around belly button level, with palms facing upward toward the sky. Imagine you have a slinky, with each end on your palms, as if you were playing with the toy. While moving your left hand up and your right hand down, feel the energy as you would if you had a real slinky upon your hands as opposed to an imaginary one. Next, lower your left palm and lift up your right palm.

Place your attention on the energy flowing from one hand to the other, as you play with this imaginary slinky. At first, you may feel a little silly. You may not be sure if you really feel the energy. Are you wondering if you are feeling anything at all? This is new to you. Don't get discouraged. No matter how subtle these sensations might feel in the beginning—slight tingling, pulsing, heaviness, lightness, prickly sensation, throbbing, feeling heat or coolness—these are all indicators of your connection to this source energy.

Keep doing this and place your attention on feeling the energy shifting from one hand to the other while you alternately raise and lower your palms. You will become more aware of the energy with practice as you play with the *energy slinky*.

Focus Your Attention

Another way to connect with the energy is just by placing your attention on your hands. All it takes is our active attention to feel the energy on a particular part of our body. The energy will flow where our attention goes. So, let's focus on feeling the energy in our hands. You may feel a slight tingling sensation in your hands. Maybe you still are not sure if you feel anything at all. This is normal and expected. When learning anything new, there is a learning curve associated with it. When I start a healing session with a client, I focus on feeling the energy in my hands. This is how I bring in the Universal Energy that I will work with. As soon as I place my attention on my hands, almost immediately I get that familiar tingling sensation, and I know I am ready to start the session.

CHAPTER 9

Let Your Healing Begin

*Do not go where the path will lead, go instead where there
is no path and leave a trail.*

—*Ralph Waldo Emerson*

Now that you are familiar with feeling the energy, it is time to use the energy to heal yourself and heal others. Everyone has access to Universal Energy to heal. You have already mastered the first step: connecting with this energy. There are many ways to do this. Believe it or not, how you connect with and send the energy is a personal preference—what feels right for you. You can even mix it up a little bit if you like.

First of all, I would just like to point out that there is no right or wrong way to connect with Universal Energy. You can read different healing books, and they may all say something different. One book may give an example of a certain technique, and another may have an entirely different approach. Universal Energy is all around us. If you were at the beach or sitting outside on a beautiful sunny day and focused on the warmth of the sun's rays and feeling the rays on your body, you are connecting with Universal Energy. When we swim in the ocean, we feel the energy of the water and its currents, and we feel the plant and animal life around us. Why do you think people hug trees? They are connecting with the energy of the tree. Although it may be easier for us to connect with the Universal Energy being outside and around nature:

Universal Energy is everywhere and in all things.

Energy with Intention

What we are doing differently is placing our *intention to heal.* For instance, when I self-heal, I will often lie on my back in my bed, usually before I go to sleep or first thing in the morning when I awaken, and focus my attention on my hands. I like to have my arms along my sides with my palms facing upwards toward the ceiling. When I get the familiar tingling in my palms, I allow the energy to come through and just relax. I allow the energy to "travel" to where it needs to go and know that the universal intelligence will provide the appropriate healing. When I refer to travel, I am not directing the energy. I am just allowing the energy to move through my body so that I have the appropriate healing. Usually, I feel the energy mostly in the palms of my hands.

There is no standard length of time I do this. Sometimes I may do this for only a few minutes, other times I allow the energy to come through and just relax for about ten minutes or so. Feeling the energy is very relaxing to me, and I enjoy connecting with this Universal Energy; however, I don't have a daily or weekly schedule where I spend hours of my day doing this. I don't feel as though I need to.

There are times when I feel the energy in the palms of my hands, and I will mentally focus the energy on another body part and feel my entire body start to relax more. Let's say at first I focus the energy on my palms, as I just described. I feel the familiar tingling sensation, pulsing, wavelike feeling, and often heat; then I will focus on feeling the energy traveling from the palm of my hands to another part of my body.

Focusing on *moving the energy* is nothing more than placing awareness on the energy moving to another part of your body. I feel it traveling to my wrists, then toward my shoulders, heart area, hips, down my legs, and in my feet. Don't worry that you don't feel as much as you think you should be feeling. It could be very subtle. *If all you sense is an area of your body you are placing your attention on starting to feel less tense, this is the energy working there.*

Again, this is a personal preference. Other times, I may focus on feeling the energy in the crown of my head and traveling through my shoulders, arms, torso, and then all the way down to my feet. I enjoy feeling the energy traveling through my body. Wherever you place your attention, the energy will flow. It may even help you to think of the energy as a *ball of light* traveling to one part of your body and onto the next to help you focus on this healing energy traveling from one area to another.

At first (or always for that matter), the sensation may be very subtle and difficult to detect feeling anything. This is okay. The energy is still there. It is everywhere. The difference is how you place your attention on the energy and where it flows. Other times, I may focus on sensing the energy coming through the soles of my feet. This really is a personal preference of how you place your awareness on the energy to heal. Do you feel more comfortable feeling the energy moving to other parts of your body or just connecting with the energy in the palms of your hands? If you like, you can place your awareness only on an area where you have pain or injury.

Do not worry that you are directing the energy for a particular outcome . . . just relax. This is about connecting with the Universal Energy having the intent to heal. That's it. Try not to get caught up with technique or focus on whether you are feeling what you should be feeling. *You are connecting with Universal Energy, feeling it within your body with the intention for the appropriate healing to take place.*

If I have an injury, let's say I strained my wrist or my knee hurts, I may place a hand on my wrist or knee and hold it there for several minutes. Usually, when I do this, I experience a throbbing in my hand as I connect with the energy. I may even feel heat where I have placed my hand on the injured area. Again, this is a personal preference of allowing the energy to come through and feeling the energy in your body flowing to where it needs to go, whether or not you place your hand on a bothersome area or do as I described in the examples above.

What if You Have a Disability?

Some of you reading this book may be thinking: if I do not have use of my hands or arms, can I still heal myself and send healing energy to others? Absolutely, you can! We have the ability to heal with our essence. The essence of who we are is pure energy. Even if you have a physical disability, you can connect with the energy to heal yourself and send healing energy to others.

All you have to do is feel the energy coming in. You can imagine the energy coming in through the top of your head. You can imagine the energy coming in through your heart chakra, near your heart area, as I do. Feel the energy coming in. Remember, all you have to do is place your attention on the area of your body that you want to connect with the energy. The energy will flow wherever you place your awareness. Connecting with the energy is placing your attention on any part of your body that you want the energy to flow. *The energy flows where attention goes.* Every healing book you will read will have this concept because it is a universal truth. Where you focus your attention is where the energy will go. You can feel the energy traveling to different areas of your body just by placing your attention on where you want the energy to flow next.

You can heal anywhere. If I am sitting in the parked car, I may self-heal. I have sat in the sauna and thought, *It is so boring in here,* and chose to self-heal. There have been times when I was lying on the beach and used the sun's energy to heal. I would feel the warmth of the sun on my body and focus on how this feels, and then direct this warmth from my head all the way down to my toes. This is healing with energy. It is all in your attention and focus.

Everything is energy, even the rays of the sun. *All that is required from you is your awareness of feeling the energy and connecting with it.* You can do this anywhere. In the beginning of our existence on this planet, we used this Universal Energy to heal ourselves and others.

My Sick Friend Lives in Cleveland?

Sending healing energy to another person in another state or country is just as easy as if the person was right in front of you. My kids usually ask me to do a distance healing on them, and they are sitting next to me! When my kids were in school, they would call me from the nurse's office and ask me to pick them up because they were sick, and I would say, "Go back to class, and I will do a distance healing on you."

Although there were times when I would know to instinctively pick them up, I realized they might just need a break from the stress of school and want to come home. Besides, I have a couch that heals. Every time my kids sit on the couch and turn on the television they seem to be miraculously healed! I am sure others with kids have a *healing couch,* too!

Distance healing is just as easy as self-healing. It may seem uncanny that we can send energy to another person in China, but this scientific principle is supported through quantum physics. Energy can travel from point A to point B without traveling through the intervening space. This is instantaneous. Healing energy travels faster than the speed of light. Spiritual light is a different property than physical light. Spiritual light that we use for healing travels faster than the speed of physical light. The healing energy is sent simultaneously and instantly. This is why we can affect another person's energy even from a distance as if they were right in front of us.

You do not need to look at a photograph of the person intended to receive distance healing. If you want a picture, that's fine, but it is not necessary. I only need to know of the person, and I feel a connection. The Universe will direct the healing energy to the intended recipient. If you think this is strange, then how do you explain when you send a prayer for someone? Prayer is sending energy with the intent for a favorable outcome. How many times have you said a prayer for someone you barely knew or did not know at all for that matter?

Did you ever wonder how the prayer was received for the right person? We don't think about this. The reason is because we *expect* that the energy of the prayer will be directed to the intended person. We *know* that the details will be orchestrated by God (Universe, Source, Creator, whatever term you feel comfortable with), so the intended person/persons will receive the appropriate outcome in accordance with their highest good at this particular time in their life.

Can you see how similar this is to Energy Medicine Healing? Think of the healing session as the prayer (intention of what you hope for) placed into the Universe. All that is required of you is to be in a state of allowing for the appropriate healing to take place. How do you do this? By *expecting* and *knowing* that The Universe (God, Source, Creator) is orchestrating the details so you receive the benefit that you are meant to have.

As I have mentioned in the previous chapter, there is a spiritual component to the healing. God, working in tandem with the client's higher self, directs the outcome. *The healer is only one part of the equation as a catalyst for this energy exchange.*

CHAPTER 10

Our Light Team

I've learned that people will forget what you said; people will forget what you did, but people will never forget how you made them feel.
—*Maya Angelou*

I don't think anyone is able to pinpoint the exact process of the phenomena of Energy Medicine Healing. There are too many variables that convolute a step-by-step description of the entire mechanism of a person's healing. For instance, there is the *seen* and the *unseen* taking place. I mention this briefly at the end of chapter 1. Sometimes it is possible to see the healing taking place; a broken bone may start to heal, for example. We may see the black and blue color of the skin change to a normal skin tone as the bone and surrounding tissue are healing. Maybe we see an open wound starting to close and heal during the session.

There is also the unseen taking place: the spiritual component of the healing. I have had clients state that they have either seen or felt the presence of angels or spirit guides during the session. Are these spirits assisting with the healing session? Possibly and probably would be my answer. There certainly is the possibility of our guides and angels surrounding us, assisting us to receive the healing that was meant for our soul's journey during this lifetime or just being there for comfort and support. Departed loved ones may be present in spirit to witness or assist as well. The healing that is taking place is in accordance and working with your highest good on a soul level. I believe that this is why not everyone will receive the healing that they hope for 100% of the time.

Maybe there is a lesson that needs to be learned, or the soul needs this experience for soul growth and/or for the growth of others in their life. Maybe this illness is forcing you to slow down your life and take a much-needed rest. It may not always be clear why we are sick or need surgery and medications. This is life, and it has obstacles and experiences.

Another aspect of the *unseen* is the light frequency in the form of energy that is channeled for the healing. How does this spiritual light actually heal? This light frequency that is introduced during the session is a higher vibration. This source energy is *the* highest vibration. It is the vibration associated with the frequency of LOVE.

Love is the highest vibration of everything in existence.

This is the energy of God. We are from this source energy of God. When this vibration is introduced, the lower vibrations in our body transform to a higher vibration.

Our vibration is elevated and establishes a new relationship with this higher frequency being introduced.

This is one aspect of how our cells are altered. After the session, we are altered physically, emotionally, and spiritually. How we are changed and to what degree are determined by the Universal Intelligence.

We Are More Than Physical Beings

We are physical, emotional, and spiritual beings, so doesn't it make sense to utilize a healing modality that can help balance all three? Energy Medicine differs from conventional medicine because it not only restores balance on a physical level, but can restore balance on a spiritual and emotional level as well.

The way we perceive our world is different for everyone. *Each one of us has a different and unique perception of reality that is based on our belief system and spiritual awareness.* If you are optimistic and are conscious of how reactive you are to difficulties and obstacles in life, your world will seem much more peaceful and calm. It can be difficult to take the "accept and let's deal with it" approach. But look at the alternative to dealing with difficulties with pessimism, viewing the world as fearful and threatening. This type of reaction to a life experience will create chaos, strife, anxiety, and extreme stress.

It is our conscious reaction that determines if we sail through life in calm waters or a turbulent storm.

It is important to have things in our life and activities that help cope with stress such as exercise, yoga, hobbies, and entertainment. This is why we love movies and television. They provide an escape. We are living vicariously in another reality when we are lost in a movie or a favorite television show. Doing things we enjoy helps us relax and certainly makes our life more fun.

If we are constantly stressed and using all of our energy reserves, how can we have enough energy for our bodies to self-heal? You already know the answer to this. We don't have the energy to heal. We are run down and fatigued. How many times have you been upset about a fight with a friend, or trying to meet a deadline for a project at work, or involved in an emotionally draining roller coaster type relationship? Don't you feel drained? Your throat may start to hurt initially. Then you may get a cold. If you don't change the situation, you continue this cycle and develop more symptoms. Our immune cells need to utilize the energy that can flow easily throughout the body to keep us healthy.

How we react to life circumstances, our emotions, and our attitudes, all affect our health and well-being.

People Prioritize Their Priorities

People prioritize their spending on what is important to them. If energy healing is not important to you, then even twenty dollars per session will be too much. People who regularly get Botox would not think twice about spending five hundred dollars or more for a syringe of Botox, but for a healing session—no way? Because it is not of value to you. People will spend a couple of hundred dollars for tickets to a sporting event but for a healing session—probably not. Two hundred dollars for a round of golf is acceptable for a weekend expense, but if you told your spouse you spent two hundred dollars for a healing session they may hide your credit cards. People who balk at the price for a healing session do so because they do not think it is a worthwhile expense.

We spend money on clothes, nice dinners, entertainment, vacations, jewelry, sporting events, and other things that we value. Why don't we value ourselves in maintaining an alignment with balance and harmony? We will pay for medications and surgery and won't think twice when we get a costly medical bill, sometimes for several hundred to several thousand dollars. This is anticipated. We expect to pay for these services. An energy medicine session is a service as well, but people will pay more for a haircut than a healing session. The price of the healing session is a form of an energy exchange like any other energy exchange for anything you purchase or any type of service.

For those of you who do not place value on a service, then any amount would be too much to pay. If you do not value different types of healing other than the conventional treatments most medical doctors can provide, then you will not seek out another option for healing no matter what the cost is because it has no value to you. If energy healing does not resonate with you, then there are other options. Thank goodness we do have many different choices available to choose from. I don't consider energy medicine as the best or the only option; I consider it *another option* that we can choose.

When Not to Use Energy Medicine

Certainly if you have a trauma situation, you would not call an energy medicine practitioner. Get to a hospital! *If I am hemorrhaging, I don't want acupuncture!* I want to go to the Emergency Room. There is a time that is appropriate for all therapies, but trauma care should be dealt with at a hospital.

If you are having a heart attack, you would not go to a chiropractor because you felt your spine is out of alignment and affecting your health. You would go to a hospital. Once you are stable, you could consider another type of healing as an adjunctive therapy for a speedier recovery.

If you are considering having a healing session of any kind, whom should you work with? Referrals are one of the best ways to find the right person. It is always comforting to know a friend or family member who has already worked with someone. If you feel comfortable with the person, and it seems like a good fit, that is a good starting point. As with anything in life, always follow your intuition.

Healing Treatments Can Be Combined

There are any many different healing options. So how do you know what treatment will be the best for you and give you the best results? In truth, the option that you think will be best and resonate with you will give you the optimum outcome. If you believe something will work for you and are open and receptive, this is very important for the therapy of your choice to be successful for you.

Choose the form of healing that feels right for you We are all different, and what one person may prefer may not be considered to be of value for another. This is why we have choices. Keep in mind as well that any type of alternative option does not have to be a "stand-alone" treatment. *It is not the allopathic medical option versus the others* such as energy work, chiropractic treatments, acupuncture, herbal therapy, homeopathic medicines, etc. Several treatments can be combined for the best outcome. It is not uncommon for people who go to medical doctors to also see a chiropractor and possibly even schedule an acupuncture session or massage therapy as needed.

We seem to categorize alternative therapies as something to try after other more traditional treatments, such as drugs and surgery, have been exhausted. I believe this is partly due to the physicians' lack of knowledge and acceptance of other treatment options that exist. Let's face it; doctors know what they learn in medical school and subsequent hospital training. Unless they are a naturopathic doctor or other alternative medicine practitioner, they have not been educated on all the different treatments available.

Your doctor is working with the tools he/she has been given to use and has been trained on. This includes a lot of prescription drugs for symptoms and diagnostic tests, such as lab tests and imaging procedures, to determine what is going on with the body. Your physician wants to do what is in your best interest. And if he/she has no knowledge or experience with another form of healing, how can you expect that they will offer this as a choice? If your caregiver is not familiar with another type of healing, they will not recommend this for you. Most physicians have not even had the opportunity to experience any other type of healing other than taking a prescription drug or having a surgical procedure.

Just because the physician who currently treats you is not familiar with other types of healing does not mean they are not effective.

Again, you have a choice to use one or more healing therapies. If you are treated for an illness or recovering from surgery and have a desire to include additional healing treatments, this is your option. It is good to have a variety of options that we can choose from to assist in our recovery and healing.

Does This Come with a Guarantee?

People want to know if I can guarantee that they will be healed of all their afflictions. "Are you under a doctor's care?" I'll ask. The answer is usually "yes."

"Do you ask your doctor when you see him before every visit if he can guarantee that you will be healed?"

"NO?!"

"Then why ask me this?" If the person is still on the phone with me, I will continue the conversation and explain, "If anyone says they can guarantee you will be healed of anything or everything, do you know what should do? RUN!" When was the last time you went to your doctor, and he said, "If I don't cure your diabetes, you can get your money back. If I don't cure your cancer, you'll get a full refund. If your high blood pressure isn't cured, your next visit is free!"?

Never!! Even medical doctors know that in the field of medicine there are no guarantees of how an individual will heal.

A true healer does not guarantee that you will be healed of anything. Legitimate healers understand that they are not healing anyone, but instead restoring harmony and balance to the body. I do not heal anyone. All healings come through God/Universe/Source—whatever term you prefer. When we are balanced, we don't have sickness and disease.

We are working with Universal Energy, which is source energy. Often when working with this healing energy, there are more questions than answers. We can't say this is absolutely true in all cases with energy healing. We can't say, for example, that energy medicine works on these certain illnesses and not on others. Working with source energy is a unique healing for that particular individual, especially since it is not just a physical but also a spiritual and emotional healing. Our life plan also determines what we will experience. There are no absolutes and no guarantees.

We could say the same thing about our current allopathic medicine. It's because even in conventional medicine, there are other unseen factors coming into play. Two people can take the same medication: one is cured and the other dies of the condition. This happens in surgery as well. Two patients go into the hospital for the same minor surgical procedure with the same surgeon on the same day. One patient dies on the operating table while the other flies through the surgery with no complications whatsoever. These unseen factors are not just inherent to energy medicine. The difference in alternative healing techniques is that we acknowledge the unknown. We know that we can't explain all that is happening.

Also, medical doctors are used to treating illness by suppressing symptoms, not eradicating the root cause of the disease. People have an expectation of taking a prescription drug, usually multiple drugs to help to control their symptoms, possibly for a lifetime. The expectation is to use modern medicine to feel better by controlling the symptoms, not cure disease. What do we have cures for? We don't even have a cure for the common cold. This is the bottom line for any type of healing you choose: *There are no guarantees in healing. There are no guarantees in medicine.*

SECTION II

....

AWARENESS

Who looks outside, dreams; who looks inside, awakes.
—Carl Gustav Jung

....

CHAPTER 11

Conscious Creation

Imagination is Everything. It is the preview
of Life's coming attractions.

—*Albert Einstein*

How Do We *Consciously Create* Our World?

At the beginning of chapter 2, I pointed out that it was Albert Einstein who showed us that Energy = **m**atter (E=mc2). The important point of this equation is that the *Energy* came first. *The Energy created form.* Our thoughts are real energy. The energy starts forming around the thoughts that we have. This is how we create our reality.

Now that you have a better understanding of energy after reading section I ENERGY, let's use this knowledge to have the energy working for us in a way that we will benefit. We know energy is always moving. We know energy responds to our expectations. We know our thoughts are energy. So, what will happen if we start expecting great things to happen for us in our life? We know energy moves. Will the energy start moving toward these new desires for the good things we want, like a new car or a better job? How about a new house on the beach, or maybe even winning the lottery?

Since the book *The Secret* first came out several years ago, many of us are familiar with how our thoughts create our reality. It is quite common nowadays to hear people say, "You shouldn't put that energy into the Universe," or "The Universe will manifest what you think," or " I'm putting good energy toward getting that job I interviewed for."

When I was a kid, no statement ever had the word *Universe* in it unless you were studying the solar system. People didn't talk like this. We didn't have this awareness at the time. A decade ago, this kind of talk would be unheard-of. People would have laughed at you! Now, people nod and shake their head in acknowledgment. Because they do this, too! They get it!

What ARE Your Thoughts?

If you know your thoughts create, isn't it a good idea to first determine what kind of thoughts you are having during the day? After all, we are not aware of every thought we have around the clock. We have other things to pay attention to. What we do have are dominant thoughts. These are the recurring thoughts and thought patterns that seem to be our usual way of thinking. You can think of this as your *default* thoughts. When you are not paying attention to what you are thinking about you have a natural default mode.

Unfortunately, if you only function on default mode, your life will be on autopilot. You are along for the ride and not doing anything to determine where you are headed.

Conscious Creation is taking your mind off autopilot and taking your creative power back.

Our mind is working like a computer program. We program the thoughts, and these thoughts will keep repeating until we change the program. Do you realize that the thoughts we have today are similar to the thoughts we had yesterday, and will most likely be the same thoughts we will have tomorrow? You will run the same mind program until you make a conscious effort to change how you think. The first step is to be *aware* of how you think to change the program.

If you are still unsure of what kind of mind program you are running, sit quietly for a few minutes. Start thinking about what your thoughts are as soon as you wake up in the mornings. Do you dread the day or are you excited about how your day will unfold? If every day, or most days, you start the morning thinking: *my life sucks; the kids drive me crazy; the car needs to be fixed; I hate my job* . . . write this stuff down. This will help you to visualize what your thoughts are about. After writing these recurring thoughts down a few times, you will start to see a pattern. *The most important part of this process is that you are now aware of your natural positive or negative thinking.* This is just as important as being aware of what your thoughts are about. This gives you a better indication of your default way of thinking, and you will have a better understanding of your dominant thoughts.

Conscious Creation Is Conscious Control

You will also develop a habit if noticing whether you are happy or miserable. Sometimes we think we are happy until we start realizing what our thoughts are about, and they conflict with what we say and how we feel. You may think you are happy, but if you write down your dominant thoughts throughout the day—*I hate my life; I hate my job; nobody loves me; I am worthless; I'm not good at anything*—how do you think you are happy??

You will also see a pattern of your emotions. Are your emotions a high or low vibration? Examples of high vibrational emotions are: love, appreciation, gratitude, optimism, enthusiasm, joy, and passion. Examples of low vibrational emotions are: depression, anger, jealousy, hatred, revenge, and unworthiness.

We know that we create with our thoughts, but our emotions also determine what vibration we are sending out to the Universe to create our life in each moment of our existence. Our emotions add power to the energy. *What we desire and our emotions need to be in alignment for what we want to create.*

Visualize Your Day

Start to form your day as soon as you wake up. When you begin thinking about these events, the energy is flowing toward this desire. You are now placing your attention on what you expect to happen during the day. *The energy flows where attention goes.* This is the beginning of the process of creation. What do you want to happen? If you are unclear of how you want your day to unfold, then how do you think the Universe will know? The first step in conscious creation is being clear about what you want, whether it is a job, promotion, new house, more money, new tractor, a new relationship, etc. Set a clear intention with your mind when you visualize.

You are getting the energy to start moving and creating. The energy is moving to shape the day that you see unfolding with your thoughts and feelings. The energy is always flowing, whether you are focusing on using energy to heal or to create.

Conscious creation is about being aware of the how the energy is working for you. Let the energy work for you!!

You can take a few minutes to visualize your day while still lying in bed, taking a shower, driving to work, shopping, meeting up with friends, waiting in a parked car. ANYTIME . . . ANYWHERE.

Think with a Purpose

You see, you have about sixty thousand thoughts a day. You are thinking all the time anyhow but with a purpose. You are *intending* to create what you want! When you visualize your day, act as if these events, circumstances, and situations that you desire to happen are happening in the present. *Act as if* they are happening in the NOW. FEEL the emotion as if they are happening NOW. SEE it all unfolding in your mind as if it is happening NOW. This is the *new now*! The one you just created.

The reason why this is so important is because if you see all these things happening in your future . . . that's where the energy will flow . . . to somewhere in the future. All of your desires will be just beyond your reach, off in some distant future. If you act as if this new situation or event is occurring now, the energy is moving to create this new present day reality.

Athletes Do It!

If you still are not convinced that taking a few moments to visualize is a powerful tool for creating events in your life, then think about this. Athletes have been using visualization techniques for years. Some people may refer to this as **visualization** while others may call it **imagery** since you are imagining, feeling, and seeing the situation play out in your mind.

Athletes have used this technique as a training tool to improve their skill level, increase performance, and gain confidence. For instance, let's say you are a competitive runner, and you have a competition you are preparing for. You focus on getting a good start out of the blocks, then feel and visualize your arms pumping harder and harder to gain speed and momentum. You are pushing your legs to work faster and faster. You are aware of your breathing becoming shallow and more frequent. You have an adrenaline rush as you see the finish line, and you push yourself even harder knowing you will be the first to cross the line.

When you do this visualization, two things happen. You see and feel yourself compete in the race as if you really are running in it. You **visualize** the performance, and you **feel** the performance. You are *moving the energy ahead of you* to create this image you already (possibly numerous times) played out in your mind. The energy is already flowing in this direction.

If during the visualization there is something you would like to change to enhance your performance, just alter your vision. You can do this very easily by creating and feeling a new image. Can you imagine possibly utilizing this technique for changing a bad habit that is affecting your athletic performance? You can accomplish this by making a change in your visualizations so that when you physically do the performance, your mind is ready and the energy is flowing in the direction for the newly created image.

Dress Rehearsal

You can think of conscious creation as your "dress rehearsal" or "practice run." You can rehearse this as much as you want. This technique can be utilized in all aspects of your day throughout your life; it's not just for athletes throwing a basketball or running a play on the football field. This is no different than visualizing your day or even an event you want to go well in your day.

Maybe you have an important presentation at work. Imagine yourself giving this presentation. Feel yourself doing a great job and everything going smoothly. Visualize your boss and co-workers congratulating you on a job well done. Again, these are just a few examples, even if you are going to your kid's class to volunteer or have a fun day planned with a friend; visualize what you want to happen and feel it happening in the NOW. You are creating a habit of moving the energy consciously to create what you want in your life. If you feel as though your "life is running you," it's time to create a new habit of conscious creation so that you can "run your life." Just like with anything you do, the more you practice this technique, the better you will be at developing this skill to create the outcome you desire.

Create an Energy Blueprint

By imaging the event or circumstance we want to happen, we are putting the energy first with our thoughts and feelings. This is conscious creation at work for you. Whether you call this visualization, imagery, or daydreaming, these terms would all describe *creating a new template for where you want the energy to flow.*

Many of us create vivid daydreams and feel the emotion behind the images we create. Have you ever noticed that some of the things we spend our time daydreaming about actually happen? When I was a kid, I didn't understand why so many of the situations I daydreamed about kept occurring. I just kept doing it though because it worked. The difference is now I understand what I was doing and why my "daydreams" were playing out in real life. I still daydream, of course, except now I know I can use these daydreams to create my reality. We have all seen this play out in our lives. How many times have your thought about running into a friend you haven't seen in a long time, then all of a sudden you are out doing an errand or at a party and there they are? You say, "How weird! I was just thinking about you!!!" You may have thought about calling a friend and a few minutes later the phone will ring, and it's them!

When we imagine events happening and when we daydream, we are creating a new *energy blueprint.* We are creating a new template for the energy to form and take shape. For some people, it helps them visualize by making a vision board. The purpose of a vision board is to put the desire into a physical form so that you can physically hold and look at what you desire. A vision board is also a great reminder of what you want to create. Sometimes we forget what we want to create, and then we see it in a physical form in a picture and say, "Oh yeah, I forgot I wanted that car." If you think it will help you to visualize what you want, then you can place pictures or words on a poster board, write them on a sheet of paper, create a "vision book," or even hang something on the refrigerator.

I like to place pictures in a "vision box" or a "vision basket." I have fun with this and make a game out of it. Creating is fun! Enjoy your power to create and have fun with it. You can pick out a decorative box that appeals to you as I have done. I also have a small basket that I may use as well. I'll cut out pictures of clothes or furniture that I like from a catalog, or a car that I want, possibly a house in a certain location, a picture of a place I want to travel, etc. I'll place the pictures in the box. If I want a certain event to happen or situation, I'll write down these things and place this in the box as well. You don't have to use pictures; if you have some great, if not, write down the things that you want. From time to time, I take out the items in the box so I remember what I wanted to create. Each time you focus on these items, you are giving them more energy and adding more power to the creation. It is a great feeling to pull something out of your vision box and actually see that what you wanted has manifested in your life!

Do whatever works for you to become aware of your thoughts and emotions to start moving energy toward your desire. Remember, energy moves! So help the energy move toward what you want to happen. CONSCIOUS CREATION is about *paying attention* to our thoughts and knowing we are creating our life in every moment of our existence. *The Law of Attraction—like attracts like—*is working whether we understand how it works or not. It is only when we are aware of what we are creating that we *consciously create.*

CHAPTER 12

Law of Attention

If you don't know where you are going, you'll end up someplace else.
—*Yogi Berra*

You can think of the Law of Attraction as the "Law of Attention" since you are now in the habit of paying attention to shape the energy to create for you.

Think of it this way:

- What you place your attention on will grow stronger.
- The more attention you give that thought adds power to the creation.
- Focused thoughts have more power than your general random thoughts.

- Your thoughts attract other thoughts of a similar vibration.
- You attract circumstances, events, and people of a similar vibration into your life.
- Your emotions should be aligned with your desire.

This Day Is Crap

Have you ever noticed when we start off having a bad day, most times the entire day "just goes to crap"? It's true. This is why we say, "I am having a crappy day!" So let's break down the beginning of the day and use the principle of the law of attraction to better understand why this happens, so we change this the next time it does happen. If we start out with a bad situation, we can still save the day.

For instance, let's say your alarm did not go off in the morning, and you know you are going to be late to work. You are already angry and cursing and in a really bad mood. Since you are already going to be a few minutes late, you rationalize, "*What's a few more minutes late to already being late,*" and decide to hit the Starbucks drive-thru to order your usual tall mocha.

You take your first gulp; however, the lid wasn't put on tightly, and the coffee spills all over the front of your attire. You grow angrier because you are giving a presentation today, and you can't hide a big coffee stain on your shirt and lap. You get on the highway and after a few miles you see flashing lights behind you. You are pulled over for speeding (trying to make up for lost time spent in the drive-thru line). You finally arrive to work and set up for your presentation to an eagerly awaiting audience. For some reason your computer is having issues, and you can't pull up your work. The crappy day continues like this until you are finally standing knee deep in crap by the end of the day.

Negative Thoughts Attract More Negative Thoughts

We have all had bad days that start out bad and have gotten even worse. When we became angry because the alarm did not go off, we started to panic over being late, and we lowered our frequency. So, we started to attract more low-frequency thoughts. In addition, we already started to visualize being late, stuck in traffic, rushing to set up the computer, etc. As we continue this downhill spiral of being angry, fear the consequences of our lateness, and attract more of the same low-frequency thoughts (like attracts like), our day has little hope of turning around.

We all have bad days. Not every day is going to be the "best day of our life." The difference is now even when we have a bad moment we can work on changing our negative thinking to a positive thought and visualize a positive outcome. What if in this situation, we visualized coming into to the office and being greeted warmly by our boss and co-workers? Who knows what the Universe could create? Maybe your boss is late that day too and comes into work after you! But what we do know is that low-frequency thoughts attract more low-frequency thoughts. High-frequency thoughts attract more high-frequency thoughts. We also know that when we create an image of our worst fears such as being reprimanded for lateness, getting pulled over for speeding, presentation not going smoothly, we are moving the energy to start creating these things.

How Can We Save This Day?

What could we have done when we realized we overslept? If something does not go your way, hit the pause button. Take a few deep breaths to center yourself. This allows your racing mind to relax by slowing down your brain waves so that you can think clearly. This increased oxygen also allows your body to become less tense so that you do not go in to fight or flight with adrenaline pumping, rushing out the door like a madman, driving like a maniac, in the hopes of making up for lost time. Now that you are calmer, it is time to think about your *options*.

There are two things that you know: you are going to be late for work; you have a morning presentation to a potential new client.

Once you have calmed down and had some time to think, you realize this situation isn't as horrible as you intially thought. So, you decide to call your secretary to let her know that you will be arriving late. You take another deep breath and realize, *that wasn't so bad*. After all, things happen. There are days when we leave on time and there is a car accident and we are delayed. We have all, at one time or another, experienced weather issues, construction, stalled cars, and other unforseen events that caused us to be detained.

Now you decide what to do about the presentation. Again, you do have options. One choice would be to postpone the presentation to a later time that day. You might prefer to email your colleague the presentaton to get started until you arrive. Some of you while reading the above scenario may have thought, *Good day to take a sick day*. These are all alternative actions. Once you calm down and think clearly, you are able to imagine what your day will be and consciously move the energy foward with your new thoughts and desires of how you want this day to unfold. You can't always control a situation, but you can contol how you react. The consternation and fear you felt as soon as you realized you were going to be late to work created a cascade of attracting one negative event after another.

We Don't Always See It Working

There are times that we may not initially see our *conscious creation* working. Sometimes it happens in an unexpected way. Several years ago, I needed a new roof on my house, so I visualized my insurance company paying for it. I felt how happy I was that I got the new roof and imagined the check for the full amount to cover the cost.

Many homes in our neighborhood had their shingles damaged from repeated hailstorms, and the roofs had already been replaced on several of my neighbors' homes. The estimate for the new roof was $7,000. My insurance company had an adjuster come out, and they said they would reimburse me for only the shingles that are damaged, not for all the shingles. They determined only 50% of the shingles needed replacement, so they would cover $3,500. It did not matter to them that if I replaced only half the roof that was damaged, the remaining shingles would not match. They didn't seem to care. I was bummed. My first thought was, *That didn't work. I put the energy out there . . . blah, blah, blah.*

The crew of roofers showed up early in the morning as I was leaving for work. Late afternoon my sister called me and screamed, "You need to get home right now!! Get home!" I thought my house burned down! She was so frantic! "The roofers put on the wrong roof!! They are almost done with your house!!!"

I drove home, and sure enough, the crew was on my roof. And when I looked up, I could not believe what I saw. It was the wrong shingle! I didn't pick this roof. There was no way to get this wrong. I picked the same roof my two neighbors had. I even picked the same roof my sister had next door from the same roofing company!

I called the owner of the roofing company, and he met me at the house. He got there about an hour later, and the mistaken roof was completely finished. I was not happy, to say the least. "I am not paying for this roof!" I repeated again and again. "They will just have to take this roof off tomorrow and put up the roof I picked out!!!"

"Let's talk about this." Thank goodness he was calm, and continued with, "It is a beautiful roof! It's even an upgraded shingle and more expensive than the one you picked out. How about I give you a huge discount, and you only owe me $3,500?"

I looked up at the roof. It was absolutely stunning! The mistaken roof looked so much better with the paint color of my house than the one I actually picked. Once I got over the initial anger of "That's not my roof!!" I really loved it!

Thank goodness they messed up. To this day, when I drive up to my house, I notice the roof and just laugh. I am so glad I do not have the "copycat" roof I initially picked. I signed the $3,500 check from the insurance company over to the owner. I did get my new roof completely paid for 100% by the insurance company!

Are You Sabotaging Your Creation?

If you say you want a promotion at work, but your feelings are that you don't want the extra workload and responsibility, you are sending mixed signals. How is the energy going to start forming around what you want if you don't even know what you want? Are you sabotaging what you really want with your feeling of not wanting a higher-level position? You may say you want one thing, but if your emotions tell a different story, and your actions are not in alignment with what you think you desire, you will not manifest what you want.

You cannot fake your intention to the Universe.

Even if we don't verbalize our thoughts, our vibration of what we want, along with the vibration of our emotions, are being sent and received throughout the Universe. When we speak our intent, we are giving it energy. Whether we speak, write about, or feel the emotion of what we desire, we are giving energy to what we want. When we imagine (daydream or visualize), we are also giving energy to our desires. We are constantly projecting to the Universe through our vibration of what we want to attract even when we are silent. What you say, what you do, and what you feel should all be in alignment for you to be in a *receiving mode* for what you intend to create.

Uh Oh . . . I Had a Negative Thought

Now that we are aware that our thoughts create our reality, it may seem scary to think we had a negative thought. *Is this going to happen??! I want to take it back!* We may be thinking. There is certainly no need to panic. We all have negative thoughts throughout the day. Things don't happen that quickly. It is your constant attention on an idea that gives it more power. If you are persistent in your attention to it, you will add intensity and speed to your creation. So if you want to *cancel* a negative thought, the way to do this is to *replace* it with another thought. In actuality, you don't cancel it; you created the thought you had. It still exists. What you are doing is *shifting your attention from that thought to a new thought.* Universal Law dictates how this works: Energy flows where attention goes. The energy is now flowing where your new attention is going: to your new thought! The previous one is no longer active.

The vibration of our feelings and emotions become stronger and stronger as we continue to focus our attention on them. With less attention, the vibration of the idea is weaker and has less creative power. When you place no attention on a previous thought, it is now inactive. Not every thought is going to culminate into a reality. When we repeatedly focus on the same things over and over, they become dominant in our minds. The most important point to be aware of is: if your dominant thoughts are low vibrational, negative ones, then you will attract circumstances with a similar vibration. You will not have a high enough vibration to attract all the wonderful things that you desire since *like attracts like.*

Do not feel guilty and beat yourself up about having negative notions. We all do. We are not perfect and happy and upbeat all the time. Remember, we are having a human experience, and this is all part of this experience. It is certainly healthier to acknowledge your thoughts and allow them to enter your conscious mind than to think they are bad and suppress how you are really feeling. Thoughts are energy, and if you continually try to suppress your true feelings and emotions, this energy will be expressed somewhere, possibly as an imbalance causing illness. The important aspect: you are now aware of how you are feeling; you are consciously aware of your emotions. Honor your feelings, without guilt, without judgment, and give yourself the time and space you need to work through your negative feelings and emotions.

The purpose of creating consciously is not to deny how you really feel, but to be aware of your power as a creator so that you can utilize these tools to live a happier, more joyful life.

CHAPTER 13

ENERGY Is the
Universal Language

The reward for conformity is that everyone likes you but yourself.
—Rita Mae Brown

The Universe Talks to Us

The Universe is in constant communication with us. ALWAYS. It never stops. The Universe does not take time out to sleep. The Universe communicates to us with energy, which is the universal language. No matter what dialect you speak while you are here on planet Earth, the universal language for all people is energy.

If everything in our Universe is energy, then the way we communicate with everything in the Universe is through energy.

If you think about this, we all speak the same language. The Universe does not discriminate. The Universe is not asking if you are black or white? Do you speak Spanish, or do you speak English? The Universe is responding to our thoughts. The Universe responds to our expectations. We think. We create.

AND SO IT IS

We are a walking talking antennae broadcasting frequency. We are announcing ourselves to the Universe wherever we go, and we are saying: this is who I am. We are saying this with our energy. We are saying this with our vibration. With our thoughts, we declare what we want to the Universe. The Universe talks back to us and says ... AND SO IT IS.

You can start practicing how to consciously create what you want. It may be easier to see your efforts of creation working if you try it out on a smaller situation as opposed to a multi-million dollar beach house. Okay ... here's an example. I have actually done this! You decide to go to the grocery store, and all of a sudden it starts pouring outside. The rain is coming down so hard you can hardly see out of your windshield. You visualize getting the parking space right in front of the door. You start to feel the emotion of how happy you are that on this yucky, rainy day when you pull into the parking lot and the front space is open just for you! You express gratitude that you already have the front space by the door. "I am so grateful I have a parking space in front of the entrance." Do you know what the **Universe says? And so it is.**

It does not have to be a miserable downpour for you to try this. I have actually done this on a rainy day. I use this example because when the weather is beautiful, I don't mind walking through a parking lot. The front space is not important to me. I just didn't want to walk out with a cart full of groceries and get soaking wet! Even this one little example that I chose shows an important point: not everyone wants the same things. Not everyone cares if they have the front space wherever they go. Not everyone wants a house on the beach. Not everyone wants to be wealthy.

Gratitude Is the Attitude

Love and *Gratitude* are the highest vibrations in the Universe. I like the word gratitude, but another word you could use is appreciation. When you are grateful for something, you are appreciative. When you are grateful for something, you are thankful. So, if it helps you to understand the feeling of gratitude better, think of it in this way: when you create a feeling of being thankful and being appreciative, this is the vibration of gratitude. When you feel these emotions of appreciating something and being thankful for something you are vibrating gratitude to the Universe.

What does this really mean? When something is of the highest vibration, it is closer to the vibration of our source energy. This source energy—that we are a part of and connected to—is the energy we use to heal and to create.

The vibration of Love and Gratitude is a similar vibration as our source energy.

I Want More of This!

The reason why love and gratitude is so important for conscious creation is because when we express this emotion, we raise our vibration. When we raise our vibration, we are in a receiving mode to attract higher vibration events, people, circumstances, and abundance. *If you show gratitude for what you currently have in your life, the Universe will bring you more things to be grateful for.* This is how this works: you will attract desires of a "like" vibration. Your high vibration of love and gratitude is sent out to the Universe: I am happy . . . I am thankful for . . . I appreciate . . . I am grateful for . . . . And the Universe talks back and says . . . And so it is! The Universe provides **more of all this!** Then your continued vibration of joy and happiness is sent to the Universe, and again the Universe responds back . . . And so it is! This cycle keeps continuing over and over as long as you stay in the high vibration of love and gratitude.

When your vibration is lowered as your thoughts shift away from love and gratitude, you are offering a new vibration to the Universe and the Universe responds back . . . And so it is. This is the power you have as a creator to place your attention on your current thoughts and emotions to keep your vibration in the higher frequency range. Focus on keeping an *Attitude of Gratitude!*

Vibration Set Point

We each have a vibration set point with our dominant thoughts that we tend to go to. Let's face it; most of us are not vibrating thoughts of love and appreciation all day long. The difference between the past and now is that you are aware you may need an adjustment in your vibration to attract your desires. For instance, if your vibration set point is a lower frequency of anger, you are not going to move all the way up the scale to the highest vibration of love overnight. You can be aware of your thoughts and have higher vibration thoughts, and as you do this you will gradually move up the scale to change your vibration set point to a higher vibration.

What Are You Grateful For?

The key to abundance is to feel gratitude for what you currently have. Find things to be grateful for. Make this a habit in your day. You can do this all day long. After awhile, you will automatically be mindful of this and start doing it often and everywhere you go.

When you wake up, you can find things to be grateful for. Be creative. Make these statements things in your life that you are thankful for. You can start with any of these: I am grateful . . . I am thankful . . . I appreciate . . . and fill in the blanks. Or you can make statements about things in your life you appreciate and love. You do not need to make these declarations out loud. You can do this silently with your thoughts.

Examples are: I am grateful for my house. I am grateful for my dog. I am grateful for my job. I am grateful for my health. I really love my yard. My car is awesome! I love my socks. I'm having a great day! I'm happy the register line is short. I love this restaurant. I'm enjoying my walk. I love my kids. What a beautiful day!

As you see from these examples, you can find things all day long, wherever you are to be grateful for. If you are at the mall shopping, you can think or say aloud thoughts of gratitude. I love this mall. I enjoy the food court. This is a beautiful dress. You can do this when you drive, before you go to sleep, even while doing laundry.

Gratitude Keeps Us in the NOW

What you are doing is creating a new behavior of paying attention to your life in every moment. You are AWARE! Finding things to be grateful for helps you to stay in the present. You are focusing on the NOW. *Remember, this is where your power to create is: in the present.* When you get into this manner of noticing things in your life to appreciate, you have taken your life off autopilot, and you are in control of your power.

I have now created a habit of expressing thoughts of gratitude all day long. When I first wake up, I lie in bed and say a few things I am grateful for such as "I love my bed," or "I love my new tile in the bathroom." It does not matter what you find to be grateful for. But I notice when I start my day focusing on a few things to be thankful for, I begin the day in a better mood. I do this now throughout the day. I either think a thought of gratitude or say something aloud if I am at home or in the car. You don't have to walk around muttering to yourself all day, but I find that when I pay attention to something to be grateful for, it helps my mind to stay focused in the present. I am not concentrating on the past or constantly daydreaming about the future. I am more focused and present during the day. I also say a few things I am grateful for before I go to sleep while lying in bed.

People express gratitude all the time for things. Saying "thank you" to someone is gratitude. Saying grace before you eat is a prayer of gratitude for your food.

Gratitude Checklist

- Create a habit to intentionally express gratitude more often.
- When we do this our vibration shifts to a higher vibration.
- Finding things to be grateful for helps us to stay focused in the present.
- When we are grateful, we are in a higher vibrational state of allowing more experiences into our life to be grateful for.

CHAPTER 14

The Giant Mirror

Be thankful for what you have; you'll end up having more. If you
concentrate on what you don't have you will never, ever have enough.
—Oprah Winfrey

You can think of the Universe as a giant mirror reflecting your thoughts and emotions back to you. Wanting something says to the Universe . . . *I still don't have this.* If you say to the Universe, *I want more money,* the Universe is responding . . . And so it is! The Universe is giving you what you want, your desire of wanting more money. You can go on wanting things forever, and the Universe will respond the same way. Great! Keep wanting! If your dominant thoughts every day relate to what you don't have— the Universal Mirror is reflecting back to you, "Please continue to bring me more of what I don't have." The energy is directed on your thought of wanting money because you don't have enough. Your feelings are about not having enough money.

I want . . . I want . . . I want. . . .

If you say, "I **want** a new car," the Universe responds again and says . . . And so it is! **Keep wanting!** The vibration you are sending to the Universe is: I still don't have a new car. To want for something is to create the energy of *not having it.*

If you say, "I **wish** for a new oven," the Universe responds and says . . . And so it is! **Keep wishing!**

If you say, "I **need** a new car" . . . the response from the Universe . . . And so it is! **Keep needing!** If your air-conditioner is broken and you focus on, "I need a new air-conditioner," the Universe will reflect, **Great! Keep needing a new air-conditioner.** The Universe is responding to your expectation. You are still *expecting to need* a new air-conditioner.

If you say, "I **hope** the new swimming pool is completed by June." The response from the Universe . . . And so it is! **Keep hoping!**

In all these examples you are expressing to the Universe that **you do not have** what you desire. *You want, need, wish, and hope for these things because you do not have them.* All your attention is placed on not having what you desire, and the energy is flowing to manifest where your attention is: Not Having! The Universe responds back. AND SO IT IS! You don't have them!

Say Thank You (Gratitude) for Your GIFT

The way to manifest your desire is to express gratitude as if you **already have** what you seek. Focus on already having it and being grateful that you do. Tell the Universe you are enjoying your desire.

This is gratitude—saying a thank you to the Universe for receiving your gift. If you say, "I love my new car," "I am grateful for my new car," "I am enjoying my new car," "I really appreciate my new car," you create a feeling of driving your new car. Look at the interior and express gratitude for the beauty. Smell the new-car smell. Feel gratitude for how luxurious the seats feel. Create a feeling of appreciation when you look at the color of the car you picked out. Do you love the color? Feel how much you love it! Do you know what the Universe says to all this? AND SO IT IS!

You Are Playing a Game of Make-Believe with the Universe

The Universe does not know whether you *actually have* a new car, or you are *only imagining* you have one. The energy forms around the thoughts you created about the new car to bring it into your life. Since your attention is placed on having a new car, this is where the energy is flowing, whether or not you have the car. This is why you focus on having it in the NOW. Direct your energy on the present to create. Concentrate on already having what you want and **express gratitude for having already received it.**

Have you ever heard the phrase *"It's the thought that counts"*? We usually hear this when we give someone a crappy gift, hoping they keep in mind that it was the thought that was most important. Well, this is the same thing in the universal gifts. It's the thought that is important.

Focus your thoughts of having already received what you want and express gratitude and thanks as if you have what you want and are enjoying it!

If you desire to have more money, don't fixate on "I need more money." You know how this will go; you will continue needing more money. Create the feeling of having more money. Focus your attention on having more than enough money to buy whatever you want.

Universe Handles the Details

When you create, don't get bogged down in the details of how your desire will be manifested. When you focus on the details to create what you desire, you are again reinforcing that you do not already have what you are asking for.

Think of the Universe as your own personal event planner.

If you direct all the specific details, you are saying to the Universe, "This is the way it has to happen." When you do this, you are limiting what the Universe can bring you. Your job is not to create a mental step-by-step thought list of how your desire will manifest. The Universe will take care of the details and start the energy flowing to create the circumstances and people around what you want to create. This is synchronicity at work. You will notice more "coincidences" seem to happen to bring what you desire into creation.

CONSCIOUS CREATION:

- Decide what you want. What is it that you want? This is placing your DESIRE to the Universe.
- Focus on what you want. Not on what you don't want.
- Create the feeling and emotion of HAVING ALREADY RECEIVED WHAT YOU DESIRE. ****You are playing a game of make-believe with the Universe.**** The Universe does not know whether you are imagining you have what you want, or you actually have what you want; the energy forms around the desire as if you physically have it NOW!
- Make sure your actions and feelings are not contradicting your desire.

Remember: Don't focus on the details. The Universe is your event planner and will take care of coordinating circumstances and synchronicity for your desire to manifest.

Be Patient!

Universal Law—Energy flows where attention goes.

CHAPTER 15

Focus on Yourself

Be yourself; everyone else is already taken.
—*Oscar Wilde*

If we all realized that our true power is being able to create from our own thoughts and vibration, we would not worry so much about what others are doing. We would realize that abundance is unlimited. We would know that just because one person has a lot of money, a bigger house, or a nicer car, does not mean we can't have all that too! We do not need to worry about what others are doing. We all have this creative power. The best way for all of us to be successful at creating what we want is to focus on ourselves and not worry about what other people have.

The Greatest Gift That You Can Do for You

Focus on Yourself

This is where your power is. Be aware of *your own* vibration. When we lower our vibration, we won't attract the things of a higher vibration that we want. If you are jealous because your neighbor just pulled up in the driveway with a new Mercedes convertible, then you are only hurting yourself. First of all, you are lowering your vibration with your intense emotion of jealousy. If you believe you will never have a car like that, then you won't. It is a waste of time and energy to focus on another person.

Stop Trying to Control Others

If you are continually focused on what others have or don't have, then you have not grasped the concept of conscious creation. If so, you would realize that they are creating their reality with their own thoughts and communication to the Universe with their own vibration, just as you are. Are you going to try and control every thought another person has? Of course not! You are in control of your thoughts and emotions. You can't control how another person thinks. If one person gets something, this does not mean there is less in the Universe for you. *Remember, the energy came first, then the matter.* You are in charge of YOU. Focus on what vibration you are transmitting to the Universe to shape the energy for your life.

Creation Is Your Superpower

Have you ever fantasized about having a superpower, being able to fly like Superman or scale a wall like Spiderman? You already have a superpower! You were born with this power.

Our superpower is the power to create.

We do this with our thoughts. We create thought energy all day long. This is the greatest superpower to have. If you asked Superman if he would rather fly or be able to create his reality and have his wishes granted by the Universal Genie, what do you think he would choose? He would choose to create his reality! Superman would realize he was not choosing one gift over another; he could create his reality where all things are possible.

We have the power to be aware of our energy to bring us more joy as the architect of our own life. If you decide not to use your superpower, you are giving away your power.

Our True Power Is from Within

This is our God Force of being conscious creators of our life. When we are jealous of another person and send these thoughts of jealousy, we are lowering our vibration. As an example, let's say Roberta, a coworker, just received the promotion that you thought you were a shoo-in for. You started directing thoughts toward her of disdain, anger, and jealousy. These thoughts and emotions are of a low vibration. You are only hurting yourself when you do this. Instead of keeping your vibration high to attract the promotion that you do want, you have lowered your frequency so that you will not attract the situations that you are trying to achieve, such as the promotion and more money. Also, don't think that since Roberta got the promotion that you wanted, there is no chance now for you. This is not how conscious creation works. *One does not benefit at the expense of another.*

If one person gets a job over another, or has left the company, and you got promoted, the Universe created these opportunities in accordance with the highest good for all concerned. There is enough abundance and opportunity for everyone. Abundance is unlimited and unending. Maybe you did not get that promotion because the Universe was creating a better opportunity for you at another company where you would have the job of your dreams. This may have been the circumstance you were in the process of attracting. Perhaps the timing was off, and there was a better job that would have opened up for you in a couple of months at your current company. These things don't just happen in the workforce; we see this play out all the time.

Why Isn't Everyone Wealthy?

Not everyone with a high vibration is wealthy. Not everyone wants to create wealth. This is not important to everyone. If your vibration is higher, you will attract more joy in your life and circumstances that bring greater happiness. This does not mean that if you have a higher vibration your life will always be perfect. We all have different challenges and obstacles to overcome. We have all created a chart of things we wanted to work on in this lifetime with opportunities for growth.

Why Are We HERE?

If we expect everything to be perfect all of the time, we might as well have stayed in paradise back home and not incarnated. Why do I say this? Because life is not about perfection. It is about the *experience of life*. This is how we learn who we really are.

- We are here to learn by our experience of living life on Earth.
- We are here to awaken to the realization we are spiritual beings, and we are one with God.
- We are here to have love within our hearts and see **Unity among Diversity.**
- We are here to learn empathy and understanding—to cohabit in PEACE.
- We are here to be able to create our reality as co-creators with our God Force energy in this Universe.
- We are here to be the self-expression of God. Each and every one of us, just by being alive, is celebrating our unique gifts and talents, and our divine light within.

You Are Not Competing for SUCCESS!

Most people really do have a desire to be successful and happy. We love success. We love to be happy. We love to have more money. But do we love when it happens to other people?

Do we feel that we are lagging on the trail behind only to be caught in another's dust? We don't like it when other people are successful. *We want the success. We deserve the success. They are not more worthy.* These are the thoughts we have in our mind. It is a rarity when you have someone in your life that is truly supportive and wants the best for you without faking it. This is someone who gets it. They know that there is enough abundance for everyone. For one person to be successful does not take away from your own success.

It is entirely up to you to be a trailblazer and create your path to success. If one person is successful—good for them! Their success does not take away anything from you. It does not diminish your opportunities to achieve what you want. You are not competing with anyone else for your level of happiness and achievement. Again, **Focus on Yourself.** If this is the only thing you get from reading this book, it will be a worthwhile investment.

We want success. We just don't want others to have success. This is how the majority of people feel. You can deny this, but if you are honest with yourself, you will admit that you usually feel a pang of jealousy when you hear about another person's good fortune. Focus on your wants and desires to start the energy flowing around what you want. Don't waste any time and energy focusing on what other people have or don't have. You know that each individual has the power to create their own reality. You are creating all the time. If you spend your time and energy worrying that good things are happening to others and not to you, this is what you will attract more of.

Crab Bucket

Have you ever heard the story about the Crab Bucket? The story goes like this: If you put one crab in a bucket, the crab will surely climb out and escape. If you put two or more crabs in the bucket, the other crabs will grab on to any crab trying to climb out and drag it down to the bottom. They pull each other down, so they are all bottom dwellers. None of them will ever get out alive. All the crabs now have the same fate.

Don't be the crab in the bucket. You know what happens to them? A few of them will end up on my dinner plate with a side of drawn butter. Seriously, though, do not focus on thinking you are competing against everyone else to have more money, nicer homes, expensive jewelry, and all of those material things. The only person you need to focus on and impress is you. Do you have the job you want, the house you want, the people in your life you want? Others are no different than you. They want to be happy and have a comfortable quality of life, too. This does not take anything away from what you desire and what you can do to create this in your life. There is enough opportunity and abundance for everyone. Focus on achieving what you want. Don't focus on feeling anger and jealousy when others get what they want. Your anger is not at them. You are angry because it wasn't you. Don't be a crab. Literally!

CHAPTER 16

Power of the Mind

*The mind is its own place, and in itself can make a
heaven of hell, a hell of heaven.*
—*John Milton*

D o you know how a baby circus elephant is trained? It is restrained by tying a strong rope around its neck with the other end attached to a stake planted firmly in the ground. The baby elephant tries to escape but learns that it does not have the strength to fight against the restraint. Over a period of time the baby elephant just gives up knowing that it is unable to break free.

As the elephant grows to become an adult, the elephant had been conditioned since a baby that it is unable to break free of the rope, so it doesn't even try. The elephant is secured even if the rope around its neck is not even tied to a pole. If you have ever seen a circus elephant contained in an area with just a rope around its neck or a rope attached to a tree or just a branch, this is why. Do you really think that the largest land animal in the world weighing at 10,000 pounds cannot break free from a rope attached to a branch or a tree, or nothing at all for that matter?

The real constraint to the elephant is the restraint to the mind.

The belief is the only limitation. The elephant believes it can't escape, so it can't. Physically, of course, the elephant could pull the tree out of the ground or snap the rope and run free.

The mind limiting belief of the elephant creates a physical limitation.

As a side note, to this day, I boycott the circus due to ongoing reports of abuse of training elephants with beatings and electric shock devices. These tactics are used to break the animal's spirit so they are trainable to sit up and roll over. It is unnatural and a complete and utter disgrace to torture a 5-ton animal to do these tricks for our entertainment.

Morris Goodman

Morris Goodman had been dubbed *The Miracle Man.* His inspirational and miraculous true story was featured in the movie *The Secret.* Morris crashed the plane he piloted on March 10th, 1981 and barely survived. He broke his cervical vertebrae at C-1 and C-2. His entire spinal column was crushed. His larynx was so damaged that doctors told him he would never be able to speak again. His diaphragm was destroyed, and he was not able to breathe on his own. His swallowing reflex was severely damaged; his doctor told him he would never eat or drink again.

Before his leisurely flight on March 10th, he was a successful insurance agent who had his own company. In an instant, when his plane crashed to the ground, he became a quadriplegic with little hope of surviving through the night. His doctor said if he did survive, he would be a vegetable. Morris said that he pictured himself walking out of the hospital like a normal person on his own two feet. He would visualize himself walking out unassisted and gave himself a goal of just when this would happen: Christmas Day!

On November 13th, 1981, just eight months from when he was first admitted to the hospital, Morris Goodman walked out of the hospital on his own two feet as a normal person—just as he visualized. Morris visualized himself walking out of the hospital despite what his doctors told him was not a possibility.

His **mind expectation** created a **physical manifestation** of his belief.

The **mind limiting** belief of the elephant created a **physical limitation**.

"Once you have your mind you can put things back together again." —Morris Goodman

When Our Awareness Changes, What We Believe Changes

We all do the best we can with the awareness we have at the time. We have said this about our parents when we become adults reflecting back on our childhood, "They did the best they could at the time." What this really means is that their parenting skills were the result of their beliefs and awareness of that time period. This is why if you have a sibling that was conceived years after you, that child may have been raised completely different than you with the same parents. What changed? The awareness of the parents. The parenting skills they had used five to ten or more years ago became obsolete for them, as their beliefs about parenting have changed over the years.

When Our Awareness Changes, What Becomes True for Us Changes

Several hundred years ago, the people on Earth thought their world was flat. They believed when they reached the edge of the Earth they would fall off the planet. This was their truth. They believed it. This belief was true for them at a time when their awareness was lower. Several hundred years later, the people on planet Earth discovered that their world is actually round. This was their truth. They put their faith into this truth and believed this truth and so it was true for them.

Which truth is the correct truth? At different stages of awareness both of these truths were correct at the time. This may seem like an odd statement since we all now know the *ultimate truth* that the world is indeed round. We collectively believe this truth. It has been scientifically proven and validated and the known truth of our time.

The truth is the truth is the truth—regardless of the belief of the time.

As our awareness changes, what becomes true for us will change. Does the ultimate truth change with each level of awareness change? The answer is no. The ultimate truth that the Earth is round did not change. The level of awareness of that period on Earth created a set of beliefs that developed their truth. Their beliefs shaped a different reality. In what had been their current reality, the Earth being round was not a possibility. It was not in their belief system. This is an example of how our reality is based on our individual belief system.

When we function at a lower level of awareness, what becomes our truth at that time and what we believe collectively may not be the ultimate truth.

We Are One with God

We see this playing out during our present time period. With our current awareness on the planet, many people believe that we are separate from God. I'll refer to this group as Group A. This group believes that we are powerless, and our lives are just a collection of happenstance occurrences. They believe we are separate individuals whose thoughts and emotions have nothing to do with the reality of our day-to-day lives. Group A accepts this truth wholeheartedly. This is their reality based on this belief. Because this is their truth, their belief governs and dictates how they live their lives.

However, as some of the people in Group A experience a change of awareness, they start to believe a different scenario. This is Group B. They believe that we do have the power as co-creators in this Universe to manipulate energy on a conscious level and to be aware of our thoughts and emotions and how they affect our day-to-day lives. The people in Group B believe we can be aware of our thoughts and emotions to create a different reality. We can be conscious of our thoughts, beliefs, actions, ideas, and emotions (these are all energy) to create a life filled with more joy and happiness and even more abundance, if we so desire.

Which one of these scenarios is the truth? For the people in Group A *and* B, both convictions are true—at least for them. The people in both groups hold faith in their respective beliefs, so this is their truth. They live their lives accordingly. These truths help form their reality in their world. As a result, the people in Group A have a different existence than the people in Group B.

Why is this? Because our reality is based on our *individualized* set of beliefs. Our beliefs provide the foundation for our **individual TRUTHS.**

This creates our individualized perception of our unique view of the world.

In both of these instances, whatever the belief of both groups did not change the ultimate truth. We are co-creators of our Universe. We each have different thoughts, emotions, and beliefs according to our current level of awareness. Just because people thought the Earth was flat, their belief did not change the ultimate truth. The ultimate truth is that the Earth is round. What was true for them in their minds at their current level of awareness did not change the ultimate truth that the Earth is round.

As the awareness of the people changed, their truth changed and became one with the ultimate truth.

We ALL Live in a Different Reality

If you don't believe that we all live in a different reality based on our thoughts, emotions, and beliefs, just watch the popular reality show *American Idol*. Without mentioning any names, we see auditioning contestants who are not talented singers, but in their minds they truly believe they could be the next Justin Bieber or

Mariah Carey. I just watched a fifteen-year-old boy who thought he could be the next Justin Bieber. OMG! He could not sing or dance. But he believed he was extremely talented! He was very disappointed that he did not move forward into the Hollywood round. Is he living in an alternate reality? YES!

In his reality, he *can* sing and dance and RAP. Is he lying when he says he is a great singer and going to be a famous pop star like Justin? In his mind, these things are true—his truths. This is his reality. His reality is based on his current awareness. When he is older and has more life experience and maturity, he will look back at this time and wonder, *Why did I think I was so talented?* When we look at past situations, we often see them differently than we did at the time they were occurring. Did the situation change? No. The situation did not change. The change is with our awareness. When our awareness shifted, this changed our reality. With that fifteen-year-old's current awareness, he is the next Justin Bieber. When his awareness changes, his reality of who he thinks he is will change.

What Is True?

You are the authority of what is accurate. Just because you hear or read something from someone, possibly even someone that you consider to be a spiritual leader, does not mean it is the truth. The true authority is you. This is where your discerning ability comes in to realize what is your truth—what resonates with you. When something resonates with you, it just feels right. You have a good feeling about it. On an emotional level, you accept the information. On a physical level, you may feel a sense of calm and peace.

When information does not resonate with you, the energy coming in feels "off" somehow. You may not even be able to describe it. On an emotional level, you may feel that no way is this accurate. On a physical level, you may feel stressed or anxious, possibly even nauseous. The energy coming into your energy field is incompatible with your current beliefs. Possibly even on a subconscious level, you are tapping into your higher self, alerting you in the form of stress and anxiety that this is not your truth.

CHAPTER 17

The Ski Trip

If I am walking with two other men, each of them will serve as my teacher. I will pick out the good points of the one and imitate them, and the bad points of the other and correct them in myself.

—Confucius

I was on a ski trip a few years ago in Vail, and we skied down to eat at Mezzaluna near the base of the Mountain, right off the main ski lift and gondola. When my kids and I finished eating our pizza, we grabbed our skis that we had placed on the ski racks outside the restaurant and walked over to the gondola to head over to the top of the mountain. As soon as we got off the gondola, I was standing on the top of the ski run and could not get the darn skis on! I kept shoving my big ski boots into the binders, and they would not fit. I glanced down at the tips of the skis and noticed my name that had been taped on these rentals was not there.

I looked at the bindings again and realized they were not my settings—too small! I must have grabbed the wrong skis that were leaning on the ski rack next to mine. I rushed over to the gondola screaming for the kids to follow and headed for the bottom of the hill back toward Mezzaluna.

As soon as I got off the gondola, I carried my skis and walked clumsily in the snow with my big clunky ski boots toward Mezzaluna. I heard a man outside standing on the restaurant balcony screaming at me! I looked up to see who was yelling, and I saw a group of people standing outside the restaurant looking around frantically. "You stupid kid! You stupid kid!" The man yelled at the top of his lungs. I knew he was referring to me and although he was mad as hell . . . I was very flattered that he thought I was a kid. "You stole my son's skis! Bring his skis back!"

Now I was only a few feet away from the restaurant, and the entire family ran down the steps to greet us in the snow. "You held us up! We have been waiting and waiting here for his skis (pointing to his son). My son just bought those skis and was so upset when they were stolen. You're such a stupid kid!!"

Finally, I was standing right in front of the boy's father. I calmly handed over the skis to his son, who looked around fifteen or sixteen. "You're right!" I said, "It's entirely my fault. I should have been more careful. I was renting these skis today to demo and should have looked for my name taped on the tips." Then I said to the son, "I apologize for holding you up! I'm sure you were very distressed when you thought they were stolen. I turned right around and came back down the gondola as soon as I realized."

The man, who was livid when I first approached, was now soft-spoken and said, "Oh my God! You're not a kid . . . are you?"

"No, I'm not a kid."

"How old are you?" he asked, now staring at me trying to figure out my age.

"I'm forty-three."

"Oh my God!!" he yelled. "I'm so sorry! . . . I'm so sorry!" he repeated. "I thought you were just some kid, but then when you spoke, you didn't sound like a kid."

He now looked completely embarrassed and confused. "You're the same age as me." He spoke softly. "I'm forty-five. You look . . . so . . . young!" I realize that with ski clothes and little on my face other than SPF 70, I did look many years younger than I was.

"What kind of work do you do?" he asked, now trying to sound pleasant. He asked me where I was from, and he said they were from New York (Nothing against New Yorkers!).

"Sorry kiddo!" I apologized to his son again.

The son was very embarrassed and kept saying, "My dad overreacted! We only waited a few minutes. No problem at all!" he kept repeating to me. I could tell he was really embarrassed how his dad kept screaming at an old lady (me).

"It's embarrassing! My dad overreacts!" he mumbled as he looked down at his skis.

His father was apologizing to me as well. The entire family was now apologizing profusely. They all commented on how nice I was. His father shook my hand. "It's my pleasure to meet you. Enjoy the skiing today!"

Understanding Leads to Peace

I will always remember this situation for three reasons. *First of all*, I will always remember the sharpness and sting of his words. I felt the anger and intense hostility in his voice. I felt horrible! I didn't mind the "stupid kid" comment. (He thought I was a kid!) He basically accused me of intentionally stealing skis, ruining their afternoon, and "holding them up." I will never forget how awful I initially felt during my "walk of shame" from the gondola to the restaurant.

This is actually a common occurrence on the slopes. There are many pairs of the same skis lined up on the ski racks together outside of the restaurants and at the base of the mountain. It's not that uncommon to inadvertently grab another person's skis. Usually, you know as soon as you try to put your ski boot in the binding that it's not the right fit. For me, I was on a ten-minute gondola ride to the top of the mountain and did not put the skis on till we got off the gondola at the top of the run. It was then another ten-minute ride back down the mountain.

The *second reason* why I will always remember this occurrence is that I know the outcome of our conversation would have been different if I yelled back and directed anger toward him. As soon as I started speaking in a calm manner and took responsibility for what had happened, without placing blame on anyone else, he immediately softened. The conversation ended with Dad apologizing to me, and his entire family offering their profuse apologies for yelling and accusing me of stealing. The dad even thanked me for coming down the mountain so quickly! The situation started with "You stupid kid!" and ended with "It's my pleasure to meet you."

I understood why the dad was so angry. It originated in fear. He was trying to protect his son who became anxious that his newly purchased skis were gone. The family was uncertain whether or not the skis would be returned in a few minutes or ever, for that matter. The dad was trying to take care of his family and had no way of knowing how long to wait outside the restaurant. As parents, we want to make everything right for our kids, and it is very stressful when we can't control a situation and predict the outcome.

I was able to see the situation from the dad's perspective. After all, I'm a parent, too. I realized he was just looking out for his son. Seeing the situation from his perspective, I was not angry with him. I understood where his anger was coming from, and I had empathy for him. My calmness toward the situation quickly diffused his anger, which allowed him to talk rationally and friendly.

The *third reason* why this is so clear in my mind is that I decided if this ever happens to me, I would certainly choose a different reaction. I was on the receiving end of the shouting match and allegations. I will always remember how this felt! I kept thinking over and over in my mind while I was skiing during that day, *If this ever happens to me, I would not react that way. I will be calm and understanding.*

A Gift of Synchronicity

The very next day, the kids and I were on the bus that drops skiers off to the different ski locations. The bus had already stopped at several ski areas, and we were patiently waiting for our stop. The bus driver was talking on his radio and then said, "We are going back to one of the previous stops. One of the skiers took the wrong set of skis." On the side and back of the ski bus, there is storage where we

MELISSA MINTZ

all placed our skis before boarding. We only had a few moments after we exit to grab our skis off the outside of the bus before it quickly departed toward the next stop.

We were on the bus another ten minutes when a twenty-something girl got back on the bus and announced, "Whose skis are these? I took your skis by mistake." She looked like she was about to cry. Her voice was shaking, and her face was flushed. I looked at the skis she was holding. OMG! OMG! I could not friggin' believe it! There was a busload of skiers waiting to hit the slopes for the first run of the day. That . . . girl . . . was holding . . . my skis.

I got up out of my aisle seat and approached her at the front of the bus. I could tell she was fighting back tears. "I'm . . . sorry," she said. "I have the same skis."

As I took the skis, I saw her eyes well up in tears. I leaned the skis against the seat behind where I was standing, and I hugged her! "It's no problem at all," I said. "I didn't even know you had my skis. We didn't reach our stop yet." When I let her go, she was crying.

Through her tears, she said, "I thought you would be so mad. The bus had to come all the way back, and I was so worried you would yell at me. I knew I kept you from getting out early on the slopes!" She said between sobs. She was very emotional.

Apparently, she had some time to think about all of this and anticipated an icy and hostile response and mentally prepared for the worst. "You didn't hold us up at all," I calmly replied. "It only took a few minutes. Thank you for letting us know so quickly!"

She gave me another hug and said, "Thank you for being so understanding!" I could still feel her shaking and sobbing as I held her. "I was so worried," she said, still crying as she turned around to get off the bus.

I realized why the tears suddenly started flowing when I hugged her. It was a relief. Her expectation of how all of this would play out was entirely different. Who knows . . . maybe she had been in a similar situation that had a different outcome, similar to the one she anticipated with yelling and hostility forcing her to tears.

The entire situation was so surreal that, throughout the years, I have replayed this in my mind over and over. I did get the chance to be in an almost identical situation and to play another role. The very next day! The previous day, I kept thinking about if I were in that same situation of someone taking my skis, I would react with understanding and compassion. It was how she said to me, *"Thank you for being so understanding."* That melted my heart. I will always remember how I felt when she said that. I will always remember how I felt when I held her, and the tears that were flowing were tears from relief.

A Chance to Choose a Different Reaction

I sensed that I was given a wonderful gift of synchronicity to experience a similar situation and have an opportunity to choose a different reaction. Just what I had asked for! I also knew that when that girl had an opportunity to react in a similar situation, she would choose to react with understanding because she will always remember how she felt when she was the recipient of kindness and compassion. I knew I had experienced a pay-it-forward moment. I knew that should the girl be in a similar situation, she would *pay-it-forward* because she experienced the emotion of empathy directed toward her, not the emotion of hostility that she had anticipated. This is what brought her tears.

The dad in the other scenario also has a new awareness of how his actions are received and will most likely choose a different reaction as opposed to his previous over-reaction. *When one person softens their stance, the distance between two opposing people is lessened until they are ultimately face-to-face on common ground.* It is a great gift to be able to look at a situation with another perspective and see a different point of view. It is an even greater gift to experience a situation playing out both roles as I did. I have learned so much from this experience. I am now more aware of my choices of how I react in situations. I am also aware of how others might experience my reactions to situations.

I am reminded of this with the popular maxim: *Treat others as you would want to be treated.* I have become more aware of my emotions whenever I am in a situation where there is conflict. I now make a conscious effort to understand the opposing point of view and react with this new awareness. Each time the hostility in the situation quickly dissolves.

- Changing our perspective can lead to **understanding.**
- Understanding can lead to **empathy.**
- Empathy Leads to **PEACE.**

Do you see how being more understanding can lead to a peaceful resolution of conflict?

CHAPTER 18

A Shift in Awareness Can Heal

When I stand before God at the end of my life, I would hope that I
would not have a single bit of talent left, and could say,
'I used everything you gave me'.

—*Erma Bombeck*

One of my favorite books that I have recently read is *Dying to Be Me* by Anita Moorjani. It is about Anita's true story depicting her heartwarming and inspiring journey overcoming stage four lymphoma. After a NDE (Near Death Experience), she woke up from a deep coma, and her cancer miraculously disappeared a few days later.

On February 2, 2006, Anita "died." Her four-year struggle battling cancer had come to an end as she lay in a hospital bed. Her body was ravaged by cancer, and her organs were shutting down. She was lifeless and she slipped into a coma. "It's too late to save her," the oncologist at the hospital told her husband Danny. "She won't even make it through the night."

In a series of synchronistic events, her story has been told throughout the world. Anita called in from her home in Hong Kong to share her story on Wayne Dyer's weekly radio show that he was hosting. Wayne urged Hay House to publish her book, and he also stated he would be honored to write the foreword. The foreword Wayne wrote is so beautiful and poetic that I wanted to quote a section of it for you. "This is a love story—a big unconditional love story that will give you a renewed sense of who you truly are, why you are here, and how you can transcend any fear and self-rejection that defines your life."[6] His insights captured the true essence of Anita's journey, and he was also the instrument that helped to bring us Anita's heart-warming message for the world to hear.

What caused the spontaneous remission of Anita's terminal cancer? A shift in AWARENESS. In her NDE, she discovered *why* she had cancer, and she knew if she chose to come back into her body (she had the choice), her cancer would be healed. *A shift in awareness does shift the body.*

All illnesses come from imbalance. You are either balanced or you are not balanced. Medical doctors use the term cure. But healers see the body differently, with an understanding of energy on a measuring scale, with either balance or unbalance. True healers know that healing comes from the inside-out—not the outside-in. When we have a wound, it heals from the inside-out—not healing on the outside first with the inside to follow. If you have ever had an abscess or a deep wound, you can see how it heals inside, and the deepness of the wound fills into the surface level of the skin, and then finally heals completely.

Anita Became a "Victim of Circumstances"

In the book, Anita states, "Because of my NDE, I went from an *outside-in* view of reality to an *inside-out* view of reality." Anita goes on to discuss how with the outside-in view of the world, she gave her power away, with external events in the world controlling her behavior, moods, and thinking. "In that model, I was a victim of circumstances rather than the creator of my life."[7]

In the book, Anita discusses her upbringing in a traditional Indian family. She was brought up to believe that a woman's role is to be subservient to men and marry from an "arranged" and often loveless marriage. "A woman's primary role was to be a supportive wife and mother."[8] Having and living your own life dreams were unimportant and frivolous and looked down upon. Anita dreamed of studying photography and graphic design and traveling the world, but her dreams were overshadowed by the wishes of her parents of marriage, and studying and following the Hindu traditions. Anita felt inadequate because she could not meet these standards and would not conform to this way of thinking. When Anita was contemplating breaking off the engagement of her arranged marriage she states, "Everything I'd been doing up to that point—the way I'd been dressing and behaving—it was all an act."[9]

Her friends and people of the community where she lived were constantly judging her for expressing different views. As she states in her book, "I'd spent a lifetime judging myself, beating myself up for not meeting these expectations. I always felt inadequate. But following my NDE, I understood that these were a false set of socially determined standards."[10]

Following her new *expanded awareness* during her NDE, Anita states, "*I understood that true joy and happiness could only be found by loving myself, going inward, following my heart, and doing what brought me joy.*"[11]

Anita states that before the NDE she had looked outside for answers in books, teachers, and gurus for solutions only to realize she was giving her power away. "I found that having an *inside-out view* means being able to fully trust my inner guidance. It's as though what I feel has an impact on the entire universe. In other words, because I'm at the center of my cosmic web, the Whole is affected by me. So, as far as I'm concerned, if I'm happy, the universe is happy. If I love myself, everyone else will love me. If I'm at peace, all of creation is peaceful, and so on."[12]

Anita's words were so beautiful and poignant that I chose to directly quote much of her insights rather than give a summary explaining her new awareness following her NDE.

YOU Are Not the Ball in the Pinball Machine

We spend so much time trying to change and control our external world only to feel helpless. Anita uses the term "victim of circumstances" which is how most of us feel going through life, that we are powerless. How depressing is it to think that we have no power to change what is happening in our lives.

With this thought process, we are nothing more than the metal ball in the pinball machine being bounced around, hitting one obstacle after another until "game over."

We all have the power to consciously create our reality by shifting the focus from our external world to our internal world. Again, healing occurs from the inside out. If you want to know how you are vibrating and what frequency you are sending to the Universe, pay attention to how you are *feeling*. Your emotions will let you know how you are vibrating. Are you overly stressed, just feel miserable and unhappy with your life? Do you feel as though you don't quite "measure up"? Do you fear life? Are you constantly berating yourself? These are low vibrations. Start changing your thoughts. Do something you enjoy. Go outside for a walk, work out, read a book, listen to your favorite music, go for a drive, work in your garden, meet a friend for coffee or cocktails, see a movie, call someone you love. . . . There are so many things on your list that you enjoy doing that could elevate your mood and bring you some fun. Get going! Go do them . . . ALL of them!

Stop Playing a Role. Just Be YOU

Anita Moorjani received a wonderful gift to be given an opportunity to see her life as she created it from the highest perspective, from *the other realm*. Anita was now able to comprehend why her body became ridden with cancer, creating lemon-sized tumors and organ failure. With her expanded awareness, she understood that if she came back with this knowledge she acquired during her near-death experience (NDE), her organs would start to function normally, and her body would be free of cancer in just a few days.

What was Anita's new awareness that caused her spontaneous healing? Anita was given this incredible gift to be able to experience the unconditional love of God, the oneness of everything in existence, and the realization that we are all magnificent spiritual beings. During her NDE, she was able to sense and understand that just by being her authentic self, she was worthy of love.

There is so much more that Anita experienced during her NDE that initiated her healing after being in a coma for nearly thirty hours, knocking on deaths door as her family and medical staff gathered, preparing for her last breath. I have thoroughly enjoyed reading Anita's story. This book is a shiny new gem with delightful spiritual insights and an *inspiring story of how self-love and self-acceptance can heal.*

An Illness Could Be a Catalyst for CHANGE

Sometimes it takes a severe illness for us to wake up and see the life that we created for ourselves, with our beliefs, emotions and fears, playing out in the form of illness. Being sick may just be the catalyst we need in our life to cause us to take an inward approach to seek answers, to seek our truth. It is by realizing this truth that we can create a needed change in our life.

When we are sick, it causes us to shift our focus. It's as though time comes to a stop and your life now revolves around YOU. Things that once seemed important to you may no longer matter anymore. Your awareness now shifts. You may become aware of your own mortality. You may now become aware of what is really important to you. You may also become aware of what could have caused this imbalance within you.

Maybe before your illness, money and your status at work were most important. Maybe now, you realize your relationships with the people you love and just loving and enjoying life is most important. Possibly you are aware that you are not living your life for you, but trying to conform and please others, hiding your authentic self. Wherever your inner truth takes you, one thing is certain: an illness causes us to slow down and re-evaluate our current situation and our life.

This is why in section I, when I discuss why everyone does not have a healing, it may not be in the person's best interest at that point in time to move forward with their healing. A higher shift in awareness may be taking place through the experience. A later time to heal may be more appropriate. *There are countless stories of people making life changes and noticing their health challenges improve or completely resolve.*

Anita's journey with her cancer, her NDE, and coming back to share her story was part of her life plan. These are agreements that souls make pre-incarnation of what they intend to accomplish during the incarnation. Her experience and teaching (and the book) were a part of her life purpose unfolding at the time in her life when she was ready to do this work of traveling and educating the world.

Now do you see why it is important not to judge a person's illness? You do not know what their life purpose is or why they are experiencing what they are going through. You do not see what the person is learning by the experience and what soul growth is occurring. Basically, in this realm, you cannot see and understand the magnitude of the "big picture" of life. It's as though you are watching a movie on a standard screen television that was made for a widescreen, so you miss a lot of the picture. So now you try to fill in the rest of the action with your mind of what you think just occurred because you cannot see the real events play out. You were only able to see and experience a small section of the "big picture." This is life. We aren't shown the big picture.

The Real Message

If you only think of Anita Moorjani as the woman who "died" and came back healed, you would be missing the knowledge and wisdom she shares from her experience, the profound universal truths. *The real miracle is within her message of love, acceptance, oneness, and joy.* Her journey with a terminal illness and miraculous healing is not so much the story as the wisdom she acquired during her experience in the other realm. The "other realm," as we refer to it, is actually a higher dimension, an existence in a higher vibratory level. We, who are hearing her story and reading her book, are the participants in this journey because we are ready to hear this message and incorporate these teachings into our life.

Lucky Her

You may be thinking, *Lucky her! I wish I had the chance to see my life, make changes, and now live it differently.* The real secret of the Universe is: **This is your gift** for YOU and everyone else on the planet. Not just Anita Moorjani. You do not have to have a near-death experience to have an opportunity to change your life! Pay attention to your life as it is now, and become aware of what is working for you in your life and what isn't. Be aware of becoming the best YOU.

Do YOU Have the Courage?

If you told a friend some changes that you think would help them in their life, do you think they would make any changes? Often people would rather "not see" what isn't working in their life because they do not want to make changes. They would rather be unhappy than disrupt their life and change the status quo. Many of us realize what in our life is not working; we have this awareness. We don't want to make changes. This would require potentially "turning our life upside down." It could require changing jobs, moving to another state, changing our relationship, possibly divorcing, quitting our job, and following our dreams. It could be a self-realization that our focus has been on negativity, constantly complaining, being jealous of others, not loving ourselves, continually worrying what others think, always putting everyone else's needs first. *Living our life being fearful of "living our life."*

Often we know there are issues, circumstances, and beliefs in our life that we need to focus on and change. We might recognize the following: our job makes us sick; we try to please others and sacrifice living our own life; are in a dysfunctional relationship; surround ourselves with people who belittle us; feel unworthy of love; live in a city we hate; and are unhappy. Many of us already have this awareness, but it does not lead us to take action. Consequently, no life changes are made.

If you know the cause of your misery, stress, and, possibly, health issues, would you change your life with this new awareness like Anita did? She was given the opportunity through a NDE to view her life differently, to see her life from a different perspective through a new set of eyes. The difference with Anita and most of us is that she now incorporates this new understanding and makes different choices of how she lives her life, how she reacts to life and life's circumstance, and is now able to realize her own magnificence. She is no longer "the victim of circumstances." We all have the ability to do this.

We have all done this before. We have all made a change in our life because of a new awareness. We do this quite frequently. It could even have been a subtle change. Someone told you that you were a slob, and you realized it and decided to be a little tidier. We may have seen an educational program on television about homelessness, and so you decided to volunteer at a shelter and donate food and clothing. Maybe you had a professor in college, teacher in high school, or boss at one of your jobs, which altered the course of your career path just by bringing to your attention something they noticed that you excelled in and should explore more fully. We continually learn things, see things, hear things, or read about something that will inspire us to make a change, to do something different. This is awareness. Each time this happens you have a new level of awareness. The choice is yours whether to act on it or continue to live your life with blinders on.

We do not need to have a NDE to be given a second chance at how we live our life.

We have the opportunity in this lifetime to "wake up" and make changes with how we view ourselves, learn to treat each other with love and respect, and understand our own divine nature of our connectedness with God and all things in existence. Wake Up!

In her book, Anita states that initially she had some trepidation about going public and sharing her story, but this statement would play through her mind. It was the message she received during her

NDE from her father and her childhood friend Soni, both of whom had already passed:

"Now that you know the truth of who you really are, go back and live your life fearlessly!"[13] This is a message for EVERYONE.

The Real Question

Do you have the courage to make changes in your life? What is your answer?

Why Is Changing Our Awareness so Important?

Anita's healing came from a shift in AWARENESS. As Anita states, "The ability to see my own magnificence and to realize that the universe and I are one and the same caused my healing."[14]

When we change our awareness, we see our world differently. When we view our world differently, we have a shift in our reality.

The reality we experience is actually a reflection of our current level of awareness and because of this, when we have a shift in our awareness, how we experience life changes.

Our vibration also changes when we shift our awareness; it becomes higher. With this newly expanded awareness, we now attract things and situations of a now higher "like" vibration.

When we shift our awareness, our new corresponding beliefs and emotions change, and our body responds to these higher vibration messages it now receives. During Anita's NDE, the higher awareness that she experienced allowed her to let go of her fears, negative emotions, and self-limiting beliefs that caused her cancer. "This allowed my body to 'reset' itself. In other words, an *absence of belief* was required for my healing."[15]

How Does a Shift in Awareness Heal?

When we shift **Awareness**
We shift **our Reality**
When we shift **Awareness**
We shift **our Vibration**
When we shift **Awareness**
We shift our Body

Do you see how just changing our awareness can be very healing?

CHAPTER 19

Belief Change Behavior Change

Life is what happens to you while you're busy making other plans.
—*John Lennon*

I Hold It In

My daughter Morgan and I decided to go to the mall one evening while on our annual summer beach vacation. While we were browsing in a few stores, we came upon an ionic footbath business. It was a small space in the mall; they sold thirty-minute footbath treatments and had an inventory of two types of machines to sell if you wanted to take one home for personal or business use. I had enjoyed these footbaths before, so I paid for both of us to have a treatment. The ionic footbath helps to eliminate toxins such as heavy metals, waste, yeast, fungus, and parasites. I find these treatments very relaxing; you sit in a chair and place your feet in a small plastic tub of warm water for thirty minutes. A small amount of salt is placed in the water along with a converter that creates the electrical current. Toxins come out gradually through the bottom of your feet. The fun part of the foot bath, for Morgan and me, was comparing the nasty brown water and then trying to figure out what the floating particles were and matching them to the pictures on the chart. This was the key for the colored particles that might be floating in the tub: white for yeast, red flecks for blood clots, black flecks for heavy metals, and so forth.

The owners of this business were a husband and wife team. The female owner Edith was telling me this story about a woman who recently came in for several footbaths. Edith noticed the tub with water from Lucy's footbath really started to smell. The stink was the smell of feces.

"You could actually see feces floating around in the tub," Edith stated casually. "So much was being released from her body."

Edith continued with her story and told me that when she had asked Lucy when she last pooped, her reply was, "I prefer to hold it in." She explained that she is married to a millionaire and does not feel "it is proper to poop."

Edith revealed that the reason Lucy came into the store in the first place was because she started developing health issues and didn't know why. "Because she started to 'hold it in,' her body was so backed up with feces, the toxins were now floating around in her body causing all kinds of problems."

"I don't understand why she is afraid to poop and 'holds it in' for as long as possible?" I said to Edith, as I was relaxed in my comfortable chair soaking my feet.

"She is married to a millionaire!" she said, a little annoyed. Edith's husband came to stand beside her and listen to this conversation.

"But I still don't understand what that has to do with anything?" I said.

"She is married to a millionaire!" they yelled in unison, as if they were in the midst of the most clueless person on the planet. Apparently, the husband and wife owners and the "poop lady" all understood that you don't do anything unladylike such as pooping in a toilet if you have a million or more dollars. How was I supposed to know? Nobody told me rich people don't poop. They both walked away irritated after realizing that I was, of course, ignorant and obviously poor.

Isn't This What I Am Supposed to Do?

I did not share this story with you because I thought it was important to let y'all (Yes . . . I am from the South!) know that I heard about a woman who decided not to poop. This story is a *person's expectation of how they should act.* Obviously, this woman did not come from money so she created a perception of how she thought people with a certain amount of wealth should behave.

This story is an example about how we change our behavior to match our beliefs. We have a preconceived notion of how we should act and do things based on our own beliefs and judgments of what should be done. Edith told me that when she had explained to Lucy that her health was being destroyed because of toxins released from her colon, since she now had a backup of old feces, she kept repeating, "I didn't know I was supposed to poop every day. I never knew that was important!" Before she lived with her rich hubby, she pooped when she needed to. After the wedding, she would hold it in for a week or two at a time thinking she was being dignified.

I have to say; I bet her husband poops! I'm sure he never told her, "I'm rich, and if you marry me you can't take a crap for weeks! It just ain't classy!!" I think it would be safe to say it was not in their wedding vows, either. This is her own belief of how she thinks she should act with her new lifestyle. Lucy created a preconceived notion of how a person with money should act and she "acted it out" in her life.

I guess there isn't a nouveau riche handbook she could have read about toilet etiquette. I know I am having some fun with this . . . but . . . come on! . . . . "I'm married to a millionaire!??" This story does have a happy ending. Maybe I could sell it to Disney! The owner said she came in for multiple footbaths to get more poop out and was slowly regaining her health.

We Create a Role in Our Minds and Act It Out

All of us have had circumstances where we change our behavior according to how we believe we should behave. This is not unique to the "poop lady." It's as if we have become accustomed to playing a role according to how we think we should act in a given situation, whether it is a role of our job, our role as a parent, spouse or friend. Maybe you have a high-level position at work, so in your mind whenever you are with your family and friends you feel as though you need to keep up the persona of how you think a vice president of a company or CEO should act.

Because of this, you never really let your guard down so people can get to know the real you. If this is how you act, most likely you will have difficulty having close friendships. You will keep people at a distance because you act in a way you perceive one should act with this title. In your mind, your behavior is just as it is supposed to be; you created an image in your mind of how you think you should behave. You created a preconceived notion of how a person with this job title should act, and you "acted it out" in your life. Just like Lucy did!

Theater of Life

Maybe you are a physician, and outside of the office you feel as though you can't be playful and silly because your patients won't respect you if they see another side of who you are. You have created a preconceived notion of how a "real doctor" should act, and so you act this role out according to your belief.

Don't we have the most fun and enjoy being around the people where we can just be ourselves without judgment? These are the people we migrate to and look forward to spending time with. We feel comfortable and supported without trying to play a role that is created from our own expectations. If we don't allow people into our world and allow them to see who we really are, then we will not be able to have meaningful friendships and relationships. All of our relationships will be very superficial if we continue to hide our true selves. We will continue to play a part in the *theater of life* that we created in our mind.

Just Be You

When we stop being our authentic selves, our energy is lowered. *It takes a lot of energy to focus constantly on being who we think we should be instead of who we really are.* How can we attract what we want in life when our constant focus and attention is on hiding who we are? If you want to attract love in your life, whether this is in the form of a committed relationship or friendships, let people get to know the authentic you.

Sometimes, early on in meeting people, we try too hard to impress another person so they will like us. We become the person we think they will like. The issue with this is that as time goes by and the real you starts to show, the other person may become disinterested. It may not be because they don't like the person that you are. It is because in the other person's eyes, all of a sudden, you changed from the beginning of the relationship. The reality is: You first may have been hiding who you are, and unexpectedly started behaving like the authentic you.

Let's say you are in a marriage playing a role of doting wife, then doting mother. Gradually you realize you are not happy. You feel as though somewhere along the way you lost yourself. Your husband says you have changed. What changed? Your new awareness that you were playing a role of who you think you should be at the sacrifice of expressing your true self.

Maybe your image of what a good wife and mother should be includes sacrificing everything for your family, with a mindset of everyone else's needs come first. You have placed your wants and needs last because you thought, *This is how it is supposed to be*. Essentially, you were playing out the role of a doting wife and mother that you created in your mind. True happiness comes from going within ourselves and finding what we want in our lives and in relationships to fulfill us, not trying to play a role of who we think we should be.

CHAPTER 20

We Do Have Options

Most allopathic doctors think practitioners of alternative medicine are all quacks. They're not. Often they're sharp people who think differently about disease.

—*Mehmet Oz M.D.*

What Is Holistic?

We have heard of the word *holistic* before, usually pertaining to different types of healing therapies. So what does this word mean? Holistic therapy involves treating the "whole person" on a physical, emotional, and spiritual level. An easy way to remember this: "wholistic." Often, holistic medicine and alternative medicine are used interchangeably. I refer to holistic approaches as alternative treatments because *it is an alternative option* to standard conventional medicine. Holistic therapy is a non-invasive and non-toxic approach to restoring harmony and balance to the body. A holistic approach involves identifying the root cause of the condition, as well as treating the symptoms. Some examples of holistic therapies include: energy healing, acupuncture, chiropractic, homeopathy, herbal therapies, massage therapy, yoga, and meditation, in addition to lifestyle and dietary changes.

Westernized medicine (also referred to as allopathic) is the conventional medical treatments used predominately by Medical Doctors (MDs) and Doctors of Osteopathic Medicine (DOs). It can be confusing, but this is referring to any treatment or therapy that is considered "the standard of care" by health professionals. Usually, these treatments and therapies are based on scientific evidence.

There are many different forms of treatment options available, not just the conventional medicine treatments, which predominantly include prescription drugs and surgery. Not every therapy works on every individual, so it is wonderful to have options to choose from. I believe there will be a time in the near future where we will have more of an integration of conventional medicine with additional alternative approaches.

Using energy therapy such as acupuncture, energy medicine, sound therapy, etc. could be more readily accepted and mainstream as people now are better educated about other options. People have a choice of using alternative options either with their current treatment or to replace the traditional standard of care approach. Unfortunately, most insurance companies only cover the traditional medical approach of treatment, which generally includes prescription drugs, diagnostic procedures, and surgery. If you would prefer to take an herbal supplement instead of a prescription medication, this is not covered under insurance either. Those of us who would prefer an alternative option may not do so because it is just too costly and insurance usually does not cover any portion of the bill.

The majority of medical doctors still consider these types of treatments as "quackery." There are already treatment centers that use more of an **integrative medicine** approach to healing utilizing a *combination of standard medical treatments along with holistic therapies.* During your visit, you may see a medical doctor, a naturopath, and often a nutritionist, who will all work together in creating a treatment plan.

When alternative therapies become more accepted by medical doctors, they would be incorporated into the treatment plan followed by traditional medicine and will achieve greater acceptance. We have seen this happen with chiropractic care. It was not until chiropractic therapy gained recognition as an effective treatment with MDs that insurance companies began to cover it. Now many plans do cover a certain number of visits for chiropractic care. We have also seen this with acupuncture as well. Acupuncture gained respect in the medical community after a study showed that it helps with morning sickness for pregnant women and is effective for helping with chemotherapy-induced nausea and vomiting. In the past, this controversial treatment was viewed as the bizarre treatment with the needles that Chinese people did.

I Have Heard of Homeopathy. What Is It?

Dr. Samuel Hahnemann (1755-1843), a German physician, developed homeopathy in the late 1700s. Dr. Hahnemann was dissatisfied with the medical treatments at the time and wanted to find alternative therapies that were less harmful. Bloodletting was a common practice back then. Nowadays, this would be barbaric to open a vein or use leeches to withdraw blood from a patient as a standard treatment for almost every illness. They did not do clinical studies in that era. If one person responded to a treatment, then it was deemed to be effective.

Like energy healing, homeopathic medicine is also a pain-free and non-invasive form of healing that works to balance the entire person on an emotional, physical, and mental level. Most of our conventional therapies are a symptomatic approach to suppress the symptoms and the immune response. When we have a cold or the flu and develop a fever, this is the body's attempt to heal itself by bolstering the immune response to signal your white blood cells into action. With conventional medicine, we would take a fever reducer to suppress the fever. Instead of working with the body's natural ability to heal, you are working against the body's attempts to defend against illness and infection. Homeopathy and energy healing both work *with* the body's innate ability to heal itself.

Like Cures Like

The premise of homeopathic medicine is "like cures like." The imbalance of the person is identified, and then a diluted substance that would cause the same symptoms the person experiences is given. For instance, if you were dealing with insomnia due to an overactive mind and racing thoughts that prevent you from getting a good night's sleep, you may be given a homeopathic substance that would cause the same symptoms such as Coffea Cruda made from coffee beans. The symptoms of the patient are matched with a medicine (also called remedies) that causes the same symptoms. If a person is experiencing symptoms of watery eyes and runny nose, they may be given Allium Cepa, which is made from red onions. (We cry when we cut an onion due to the sulfur being released, not the strong odor.)

These remedies are natural substances, usually found in plants or minerals. It may take a great deal of time to individualize a medicine to match the symptoms. There may be over a hundred different remedies that could treat a series of symptoms that the patient is experiencing. Our bodies' immune system is then stimulated to self-heal to return to a normal state of balance. Homeopathic treatments have garnered a lot of controversy for their effectiveness because homeopathic medicines can be so heavily diluted that the final therapeutic dose seems to be nothing but water. The original substance, after all the repeated dilutions, is no longer detectable. Some may argue that its effectiveness then is nothing more than a placebo effect.

If we compare this dosing rationale to our pharmaceutical drugs, just the opposite effect occurs. With our standard drugs that we take, there is usually a dose response. When we increase the dose, we have greater efficacy, and usually this is accompanied by an increase in side effects as well. In homeopathic medicines, it is the smallest dose (most diluted) that stimulates the immune system to heal. The more the remedy is diluted, the greater the potency. The medicine is effective even when there is no detectable substance left in the dilution. How is this possible?

Although the active ingredient has been diluted to undetectable levels, the vibration of the molecules is still present. You can think of homeopathic medicine as a form of energy medicine since the vibration of the original substance is still in the dilution. The medicine still has an energetic imprint in the dilution even though the levels are too low to detect. The energetic imprint of the original substance is there no matter how many times the solution was diluted.

Because the active ingredient is still in the water in the form of its *energetic imprint*, homeopathy is a type of energy medicine, which some people also refer to as vibrational medicine. This is a difficult concept for mainstream practitioners to comprehend. Medical doctors have been trained that increasing the dose of a drug usually increases the efficacy. In addition, most drugs are used to treat symptoms, not to work on a whole body approach to balance the mental, physical, and emotional attributes of the patient.

Homeopathy Is Not New

Homeopathy has been around for over 200 years, but has never really caught on as a form of medical treatment. The American Medical Association (AMA) was formed in 1847 with an agenda to create a medical monopoly for mainstream doctors. The AMA claimed that homeopathy was quackery. Why? It was all about economics and whose hands were in the money jar. The plain and simple explanation is: the allopathic doctors did not want the competition.

The AMA is also the organization that shut down Royal Rife's work. "Rife," as he is known, was curing the "incurable patients" using only energy. Rife was able to determine what frequency was required for a disease-causing organism to disintegrate. As patients often flocked to see him for quick and pain-free cures, the medical community rallied to discredit his work and destroy his equipment.

If you follow the money trail you will see how our approved current medical treatments, consisting mainly of surgery and drug therapy, create a medical monstrosity limiting our choices of effective holistic, non-invasive treatment options.

Most often, alternative treatments are used as a last hope when other treatments have been exhausted. Homeopathy does not kill people. When the AMA was founded, it was the era of *bleed, blister, purge, and puke* treatment choices. Bloodletting killed George Washington (1732-1799). George Washington died after being treated for a throat infection by bleeding 5 pints of blood, which further weakened his condition. An average adult has 10 pints of blood, so 50% of his blood volume was drained. Usually, a blood loss of 30-40% causes the body to go into shock and shut down without a blood transfusion. As a frame of reference, when you donate blood 1 pint is taken.

Blistering was a treatment performed by placing a caustic agent on the skin to form blisters that were drained to "draw out toxins." Laxatives were used to purge the patient's bowels of toxins, and medicines were used to induce vomiting. These treatments seemed more like medieval torture than useful medical treatments, yet they were accepted mainstream treatments during that period of time that killed patients. However, less invasive and curable therapies such as homeopathy and Rife's frequency treatments were forced out of business because the medical associations had been established initially to create high incomes for formally trained medical doctors and the newly established medical organizations. This is why alternative treatments are not given as first line therapy and are not covered by most insurance plans. It is not due to the protection of the American people or lack of efficacy.

Our pharmaceutical drugs and vaccines all have a litany of adverse events, some are even life-threatening. They are still approved and kept on the market, even with countless deaths being reported. The adverse events for drugs are always higher than what is listed in the Prescribing Information (PI). The time duration for a drug study is very short, usually four to six weeks, and this is even the case for drugs that may require a lifetime therapy for chronic conditions. How can this be an accurate reflection of how safe a drug will be taken for a year or even a lifetime?

The PI for each drug only lists the adverse events seen during the clinical trial, and does not list adverse events after the drug is approved, unless the PI is amended to reflect additional adverse event reports after the drug has been on the market. Did you know that after a drug is approved and prescribed, the adverse events reported by your doctor are on a *volunteer* basis? This is why adverse events are under-reported. Doctors don't want to take the time to follow up with the drug companies and fill out the required paperwork to report every side effect for every drug their patients are taking. Because of this, less than 10% of all the adverse events actually get reported to the drug companies who then submit a report to the FDA (Food and Drug Administration).

We have medical plans that cover our prescriptions drugs, hospitalizations, office visits, and diagnostic medical care, but how many insurance plans do you know that cover energy healing, acupuncture, or homeopathy?

Energy of the Medicine Is Transferred to the Water

Even though the final dilution of a homeopathic remedy contains no detectable levels of the original medicine that was used, the energy of the medicine is transferred to the water. Energy Medicine Healing also works by energy transfer. The energy from the healer is transferred to the client.

There are people who would argue that homeopathic treatments do not work because they do not understand *how* it works. (This is another similarity with Energy Medicine Healing.) Many drugs are approved with an unknown mechanism of action. If you ask patients how the pharmaceutical drugs they are taking work, most likely they will not know, and chances are their physician won't know either.

We are seeing more homeopathic remedies becoming available in drugstores now. Arnica, sold in many drugstores in tablet and a topical form, is a very effective herbal treatment mainly used for bruising, sprains, and joint pain. Even medical doctors are routinely recommending arnica for sports-related injuries to reduce swelling, inflammation, and bruising. Arnica tablets have also been used to help alleviate postoperative trauma and expedite healing by decreasing inflammation. I have used arnica for muscle strains and bruises, and it works!

Water Has Memory

If you do not believe that water has memory or that water can take in information, you will not believe in the benefits of homeopathy. The entire premise of Dr. Masaru Emoto's work basically proved the mechanism of action of homeopathic medicine. His work created two new tenets: *Water takes in information. Water has memory.*

Dr. Emoto began photographing water crystals in 1994. He first became intrigued with the idea of taking pictures of water crystals after casually opening a book about science and reading something that caught his attention: "Are there any identical snow crystals?" His work and the fascinating photographs of the water crystals are featured in his books, *The True Power of Water* and *The Hidden Messages in Water*.

How did Dr. Emoto photograph frozen water crystals? He would collect the water, expose the samples to information by writing down a specific word, and then he would tape the word to the bottle. The water was then placed in small petri dishes and frozen for three hours. The samples were viewed under a microscope as light was being directed at the frozen sample of water. In the first couple of minutes, as the ice would start to melt gradually, crystals would form, and a photograph was taken.

Dr. Emoto hypothesized that the crystals formed in the water changed when the information it was given changed.[16] First, two bottles of water were labeled with separate messages and frozen. Then Emoto photographed the crystal formations. For example, when the label with the word "Thank You" was placed on a glass water bottle, beautiful hexagonal crystals materialized. Conversely, when the label "You Fool" was placed on the second glass bottle, only fragments of crystal formed.[17] The most beautiful crystals developed when positive words such as happiness, well done, and peace were pasted on the water bottles. As you would expect, the words *love and gratitude* created the most magnificent water crystals. When the water was shown negative words such as no good, devil, powerless, and war, the crystals did not form.

Dr. Emoto's work with the water crystals has shown that words, photographs, music, and consciousness change the crystalline structure of water. The water molecules have been changed with the new information that is introduced and received. *Water has memory*, and can take in information and change accordingly. Although in homeopathy where the active agent cannot be detected, the energetic imprint of the substance has *vibrationally* changed the water. The water has retained the memory of the initial substance, and so the energetic imprint (vibration) of that substance still remains. This is why even the most diluted homeopathic medicines still retain their potency.

In *The True Power of Water*, Dr. Emoto writes about how our consciousness has the ability to change water. How do you think the intention of destruction, hatred, and violence affect the condition of the water? The quality of the water will start to deteriorate. This is the drinking water we are creating on our planet. We have the ability to change the nature of our water with the intention to do so.[18] We know that everything has a vibration and leaves an energetic imprint in everything it comes in contact with.

Can a Person's Vibration Be Measured?

Dr. Emoto talks about a device he used that measures a person's energy. He refers to this as measuring the person's "hado," which means vibration. The hado measuring device will show abnormal vibrations that are causing illness. Dr. Emoto showed that water can carry information and that our body does respond to the information from the water we drink. He prepared water to carry the opposite vibration by exposing the water to new information that would cancel the existing abnormal vibration that a person might have. This would "correct" the vibration. Dr. Emoto has cured people with chronic and life-threatening illnesses with water.

We do not need to get on a plane and fly to Japan to drink water, which has been exposed to new information to change our vibration. Dr. Emoto's work is another validation that a positive shift in our vibration can help us to heal. He has already shown in his photographs that the words "love and gratitude" form the most beautiful water crystals. We can change the vibration of the water we drink by pasting the words "love and gratitude" on the glass. Since we also know that consciousness alters the vibration of water as well, we can express gratitude either silently or aloud for the water we drink. Prayer has also been shown to change the quality of water.

Basically, this is what alternative healing modalities do. **They send a new vibration to correct the abnormal vibration.** Energy healing, acupuncture, sound healing, and other vibrational healing approaches change and correct abnormal disturbances. Even participating in yoga can help energy flow and shift the vibration and help the body to heal. *There is more than one path to healing.*

We do have many options to use, even combined with any conventional treatment we choose. People tend to think of healing as either going to a medical doctor or trying some form of a holistic method. We do not have to think of it as either an alternative *or* conventional treatment; we can add on more than one modality to help us. When using conventional medicine with alternative healing, we are integrating both approaches. This is Integrative Medicine.

The method that Dr. Emoto used to heal with water is not something new. This concept is similar to how we can cancel a sound vibration to create silence. This is how Noise Canceling Headphones work. Sound is a form of energy that travels through the air in waves with peaks (highs) and troughs (lows). It is possible to cancel a wave by reversing the incoming one. Where the original wave has a peak, the reverse wave has a trough. The wave is inverted, which cancels itself. So what do we have? NO SOUND. The difference between the headphones and Dr. Emoto's water therapy is that we are canceling the vibration of sound waves instead of a vibration causing illness.

Pilots wear Noise Cancelling Headphones and many passengers now wear these on flights to tune out the loud engine. How do these headphones work? They have a microphone, which picks up background noise and the electronic circuitry processes the noise and inverts the wave to cancel the sound coming through the ear speakers. It is the same scientific principle used for the healing water as the silencing of sound. An opposite wave cancels the original wave.

Royal Raymond Rife

Royal Rife was one of the most gifted and brilliant scientists of this century. He was born on May 16, 1888, and died August 5, 1971. Rife invented the "Universal Microscope" that allowed him to view microorganisms (usually a virus and bacteria) while they were still alive. The microscope used at this time was the electron microscope, which used chemicals to stain the microbes, killing them instantly. Rife was the first person to view the microbes alive and in their natural state. This was the first time this was ever accomplished!!

Rife had studied optics at the leading optical industry in Germany for six years. His creation of the Universal Microscope, which he presented in 1933, was pure genius. It had nearly 6,000 parts and weighed around 200 pounds. His microscope was able to magnify objects 60,000 times their actual size!

Rife discovered that each microbe resonated at its own unique frequency. He would observe the microbe through the microscope, and when bombarded with the matching frequency, the cell would usually explode, (devitalize was the term Rife used) leaving the healthy cell unharmed. (An example of this would be the opera singer being able to shatter a wine glass when singing a note that is of the same frequency.)

It took Rife many hours of looking in the scope searching for the correct frequencies to destroy the disease-causing microbes. His research took years to determine and log these corresponding *resonant frequencies* (naturally occurring vibration) that would destroy the pathogen while being able to view them exploding under the magnification of his scope. He invented the "beam ray" machine to zap the microbe with the resonant energetic frequency so that it would self-destruct, or at least weaken the cell so that the immune system could finish the job.

According to Rife and many of his supporters, his beam ray machine cured them of illnesses and terminal diseases that conventional medicine was unable to alleviate. Many patients whose doctors had deemed "hopeless" and "incurable" were completely healed with the Rife frequency device. There were testimonials and documentation of patients with cancer, lupus, tuberculosis, infections, and many other life-threatening diseases, who returned to normal health after being treated with the Rife healing device.

Rife was curing cancer in the 1930s. You would think that he would have been exalted as a hero at the time with files of documented case histories of curing the "incurable." He was actually persecuted by his colleagues and the American Medical Association (AMA). Due mostly to greed and jealousy of his associates, his work was labeled "quackery" and "unproven." After all, Rife was curing cancer without costly therapies and drugs. He only needed to use his electronic device to generate the corresponding resonant frequency of the pathogen causing illness or injury. Instead of the invasive and painful treatments of surgery, radiation, and chemotherapy, he only needed a small amount of energy to effectively destroy or weaken the cells. Most of his equipment and research data was stolen and destroyed. Roy Rife died at 83, alone and broke, his reputation tarnished, and his life's work expunged.

The Rife technology and machines are still used today, but little of it resembles the original Rife beam ray device using his frequency settings, since most of his equipment and research records were confiscated and destroyed. It is questionable whether the results that Rife achieved could be replicated with the current frequency healing devices on the market today.

Rife proved with his Universal Microscope that cells have a unique signature energy frequency. When in actuality, everything in existence vibrates and has a corresponding energy frequency. This is why using vibration and frequency is effective in healing; whether it is sound therapy, energy medicine, or even the vibration of water as in Dr. Emoto's work. Every cell, organ, and structure of our body vibrates and has its own resonant frequency, which responds to the *new frequency* being introduced. Even the subtle frequencies of our modern technology such as microwave ovens, cell phones, computers, televisions, and even power lines can affect our health by *shifting our vibration.*

Our bodies are electrical, so we react and absorb the frequencies we are exposed to. This is why when we experience an electric shock or are hit by a lightning bolt, our bodies react to a "power surge" and can stop functioning. Our heart beats by using electrical signals, which is why a defibrillator is used to send an electric shock to restart the heart when someone goes into cardiac arrest.

Roy Rife was able to reproduce the frequency of the virus, causing it to vibrate and ultimately shatter, just like an opera singer hitting the note corresponding to the frequency of the wine glass. When Rife had a frequency match to the virus, the healthy cells were unaffected and unharmed. Just as in the glass shattered by the singer, the rest of the objects in the room were unaffected and remained intact. Next time you are out with friends and enjoying a glass of wine say "cheers" and clink your glasses. Take a moment to listen to the sustained ring of the glass. When the glass is bumped, it vibrates creating a tone. This tone is the resonant frequency of the glass!

How Can This Happen?

You may think to yourself, *How could this happen?* A simple pain-free, non-invasive approach to curing disease and alleviating symptoms of even the "incurable" and restoring health and vitality, even offering hope to the terminal patients? How can this technology be destroyed and deemed quackery and unethical to use? Rife was curing people with ENERGY. That's it! This concept may seem like something out of a Stephen Spielberg thriller—how the human race is subjected to the most gruesome and painful procedures and a lifetime of multiple drugs only to suppress symptoms, while simple, non-toxic therapies are deemed illegal for us to use and the information of their success is hidden from us and suppressed.

Do you think this suppression ended with the Rife technology? Very little has changed since then. Other less invasive and less costly options are being hidden from us today. It's about money, politics, and power. If you were a medical doctor who treated allergies and someone came up with a simple cure for treating all allergies, would you be happy? The medical doctors in power at the time realized the potential of this technology would be very costly to their livelihood.

Do you not think this is still happening? Read on. . . .

CHAPTER 21

Why Are Alternative Treatments "Alternative"?

Doctors are men who prescribe medicines of which they know little,
to cure diseases of which they know less, in human beings
of whom they know nothing.
—Voltaire

Why are these "alternative" treatments alternative anyway? The treatment paradigm should be *reversed* with these non-invasive and non-toxic therapies *given first*. Then, if these options do not provide a benefit, more invasive and aggressive medical intervention should be given. Nowadays, the treatment plan is usually starting with the most aggressive therapies, then utilizing a simpler alternative approach as a "last hope."

Why do our treatment plans seem to be from a backward to forward approach?

Do your own research and you will see a pattern of how our current healthcare functions with a "cradle to grave" mentality: get individuals on vaccines and drugs from "baby to death" to create a lifetime of revenue for our medical practitioners, drug companies, and other medical and government affiliations. Don't blame your doctors; they are doing their best with the options they are given to use. Much knowledge of success and cures with alternative treatments is being suppressed and withheld. Holding your healthcare practitioner accountable would be like blaming a carpenter for not making a sturdy chair after only given enough wood to make a three-legged chair.

Your physician is providing the best care in accordance with their medical training and the tools they have been given to use. Our healthcare practitioners are most likely as frustrated as you are with limited options available to help ease their patients suffering. Medical doctors are also the unknowing victims of this political and medical monopoly that is limiting their education and knowledge, providing misinformation, and reducing the availability of other viable treatments and therapies.

I included the information in this chapter so that you would be able to see for yourself how these government and medical organizations that are supposedly looking out "for *our* best interest" may very well be looking out for "*their* best interest." And they are doing so under the guise of "our protection." The intent of this information that I have provided for you in this chapter is to *awaken you to see a situation from a new perspective* in order to see the big picture of why you have limited options with your healthcare and your individualized approach to wellness. After all, being aware does create a shift in your perception.

The "Health Ranger"

There is a website that I enjoy reviewing: www.naturalnews.com. You can sign up with your email address and receive daily updates. This website was created by Mike Adams, who refers to himself as the "Health Ranger." Mike is a consumer health advocate and award-winning journalist. I have found his work informative, well researched, with up-to-date cutting edge science and medical articles, including natural healing and nutritional information. Sign up! Mike has done the research for you to bring you the latest in natural health news.

Claiming Cherries Are Good for Us Is a Crime in America

The FDA sent certified warning letters to cherry farmers for posting claims on their websites claiming that tart cherry juice concentrate helps with arthritis, gout, diabetes, and may possibly prevent cancer. Most of these farmers were in Michigan, which is the largest producer of tart cherries in the United States.

For the farmers to make these claims, according to the FDA, the cherries need to be registered as a drug. To make health claims about any food is considered "drug promotion," and this is illegal in America to market an "unapproved drug." What would registering cherries as a drug entail? To register the cherry as a drug would cost millions of dollars to fund the clinical trials necessary to collect the required efficacy and safety data, then file a new drug application with the FDA as part of the approval process. It would also take many years to complete all the required clinical trials.

The warning letters state that if the cherry farmers do not comply with their regulations and correct these violations, this may "result in enforcement action without further notice." The farmers were given 15 days to respond in writing after the receipt of the letter of the steps taken to comply with the FDA regulations. Doesn't it seem like a waste of time and money for the FDA to protect us from a pain-free-effective-*zero death* treatment?

Death by Cherry Pie?

This is why we don't know about all the healing benefits of foods, herbs, and vitamins. The information is suppressed due to fear that their companies would be shut down and be criminally prosecuted by the FDA. They are protecting their own financial interest and the pharmaceutical industry. After all, who croaked on a cherry? Have you ever read an obituary that said, "It was the cherry pie that killed him? The rest of us ate the pumpkin pie with whipped topping!"?

The farmers were touting documented scientifically validated truth. The benefits of tart cherries have been studied and researched since the 1950s. Tart cherries are different from the sweet cherries (usually sold in stores) and can be identified by their bright red hue. Tart cherry juice has even been documented to help with insomnia and improve the amount of sleep time. Cherries contain melatonin, which helps people to sleep better at night. Tart cherries contain a much higher content of melatonin than sweet cherries.

The dissemination of these truthful and documented scientific claims should be protected as freedom of speech under the First Amendment. The FDA censors truthful information while protecting the corporations who pay their fees. This is a flagrant breach of public trust and contrary to our rights for freedom of speech. They are not being held accountable for any wrongdoing.

Pomegranate Juice Effective for Prostate Cancer

Pomegranate juice has shown to be effective in slowing prostate cancer. This research was presented in 2009 at a scientific meeting of the American Urological Association (AUA). This was a long-term study that started in 2003 and followed 48 participants over six years. This study showed that drinking 8 ounces of pomegranate juice daily slowed the progression of prostate cancer. In addition, there were no serious adverse events.[19]

This is another example of the healing benefit of food that we don't hear about because it is illegal to disseminate this information to the public. The FDA sent a warning letter to the pomegranate juice company, POM Wonderful, for referencing this clinical study on their website. The company's website contains excerpts from numerous medical and scientific journals regarding various health benefits of pomegranate juice. According to the FDA, the mention of these scientific publications was evidence of the product's intended use as a drug. POM Wonderful is not wonderful at all as they are illegally trying to sell an unapproved drug. The verbiage is the same as the other warning letters such as "The therapeutic claims on your website establish that these products are drugs."[20] Again, like the other companies, their crimes consisted of stating excerpts from scientific research and clinical studies published in peer review journals. The FDA considers this unlawful marketing that has the consequences of misleading the public. POM Wonderful didn't say, "Drink this juice. It cures prostate cancer."

If a man decides to drink 8 ounces of pomegranate juice or to take pomegranate extract daily to lower the PSA (prostate-specific antigen) levels based on scientific research, how can this be illegal for a company to use an excerpt from the clinical study that supports this claim on their website? Educating people on the benefit of a food that has been researched, validated by scientific proof, with documented results published in a medical journal, should not be against the law.

We Aren't Allowed to Know What Is Good for Us

Legally, our herbs, vitamins, and natural substances can't claim to do anything. I'm surprised the label on the bottle doesn't read, "Just take one—see what happens." Don't just blindly believe everything because you read it in a book or heard about it somewhere. Always search for your own truth. Again, follow the energy trail (in this case—money trail) and it will lead you to the truth.

Will people who eat these healing foods have nerve disorders, heart failure, paralysis, rashes, coma, and death? Vaccines and prescriptions drugs have all caused these adverse events. We are not protected from these side effects, but we are protected for "our own good" regarding the benefits of benign, innocuous healing foods that provide us with vital life force energy to maintain the balance and harmony of the body. These healing foods work with the body's innate healing power and do not have adverse events causing irreversible damage as we have seen with many approved prescription drugs.

Broccoli has been studied at University-based hospitals and cancer research centers for years regarding the anti-cancer chemicals found in fresh broccoli. Claims cannot be made stating that broccoli may have anti-cancer benefits or may protect against cancer because this would be making a claim about treating a disease. Only an FDA approved drug can make statements of preventing, treating, or curing a disease. Therefore, our foods, just like the tart cherries used for inflammation and gout, cannot legally make a claim to treat a specific disease.

Broccoli sprouts have shown to have 20-50 times the anti-cancer fighting potential than the actual broccoli heads. One ounce of broccoli sprouts contains more of the cancer-fighting chemical sulforaphane than two pounds of broccoli. If you can't stand the bitter taste of broccoli, eat the sprouts. They taste great added to a sandwich or salad. The best way to eat broccoli stems to gain their health benefits is to eat them lightly sautéed or raw. Overcooking by boiling can destroy the cancer-fighting compounds. There...I said it ...and I did not spend millions on a clinical study. My warning letter may be in the mail. It's not as though the food industry is stating we know for a fact that broccoli can offer a protective benefit or cure cancer. This cannot even be implied legally for our own good.

According to the standards of the FDA, when a drug causes heart attacks, paralysis, brain damage, coma, and even death, this is an acceptable risk every time we take our approved FDA drugs. By the way, have you noticed that the television commercials for our prescription drugs have become more entertaining? When the moderator has to state the side effects of the drug, we aren't really paying attention to how severe they are. We are focusing on the visual in the commercial, not listening to the litany of adverse events.

What kind of adverse reactions are we going to see with cherries, pomegranate juice, broccoli, walnuts, and all the other foods that have shown to be beneficial in disease prevention? These healing foods are a part of preventing disease, which is quite different from visiting a doctor for tests done to see if you have a disease. What did you do to *prevent* it? You just found out if you have something wrong or not.

Walnuts Are Illegal Drugs Too

The FDA has also referred to walnuts as illegal drugs. The FDA sent a letter to Diamond Foods after they posted truthful information regarding the health benefits of walnuts on their website. This is one of the claims that was posted on Diamondfoods.com and stated on the FDA warning letter.

"Studies indicate that the omega-3 fatty acids found in walnuts may help lower cholesterol; protect against heart disease, stroke, and some cancers; ease arthritis and other inflammatory diseases, and even fight depression and other mental illnesses."[21]

The FDA letter contained verbiage such as "your walnut products are drugs" and they may not be marketed "without an approved new drug application."[22]

This section of the FDA letter made me laugh.

"Additionally, your walnut products are offered for conditions that are not amenable to self-diagnosis and treatment by individuals who are not medical practitioners; *therefore, adequate directions for use cannot be written so that a layperson can use these drugs safely for their intended purposes.*"[23]

Where are the friggin' directions? The walnuts do not come with adequate directions for a layperson such as myself to self-medicate. I have to remind myself every day when I go to the grocery store that I that I did not go to medical school. I have not been sufficiently trained for such life or death decision-making. What if I overdose by eating seven walnuts when I only needed five? There are over thirty peer-reviewed journals that support the claims that Diamond Food posted on their website. The studies showed that walnuts protect the heart and reduce cholesterol.

Documented FDA Suppression

Even Congress recognizes the problems with the FDA suppressing proven, researched, and published information. On November 10, 2005, a bill called The Health Freedom Protection Act was introduced to prohibit the FDA from the suppression of documented, truthful information. This is an excerpt from the speech by Texas Congressman Ron Paul, introducing the bill in the United States House of Representatives. This introduction documents the transgressions of the FDA against the American people.

"Because of the FDA's censorship of truthful health claims, millions of Americans may suffer from diseases and other health care problems they may have avoided by using dietary supplements. For example, the FDA prohibited consumers from learning how folic acid reduces the risk of neural tube defects for four years after the Centers for Disease Control and Prevention recommended every woman of childbearing age take folic acid supplements to reduce neural tube defects. This FDA action contributed to an estimated 10,000 cases of preventable neural tube defects!

The FDA also continues to prohibit consumers from learning about the scientific evidence that glucosamine and chondroitin sulfate are effective in the treatment of osteoarthritis, that omega-3 fatty acids may reduce the risk of sudden death heart attack, and that calcium may reduce the risk of bone fractures.

The Health Freedom Protection Act will force the FDA to finally comply with the commands of Congress, the First Amendment, and the American people by codifying the First Amendment standards adopted by the federal courts. Specifically, the Health Freedom Protection Act stops the FDA from censoring truthful claims about the curative, mitigative, or preventative effects of dietary supplements, and adopts the federal court's suggested use of disclaimers as an alternative to censorship. The Health Freedom Protection Act also stops the FDA from prohibiting the distribution of scientific articles and publications regarding the role of nutrients in protecting against disease."[24]

Sickness Generates Revenue

When I was a kid, there were gas stations on every street corner. Now, it seems as though I drive along and see one pharmacy after another. We have a pharmacy in the grocery stores, department stores, and in many medical office buildings. The pharmacies do a great deal of business. People are sick and need their medication. The doctors' offices are so crowded that when I am working and calling on my customers, I can barely find a parking spot. The waiting rooms are packed, and you may have to wait an hour or more. Our healthcare system seems to function more like a sick care system. After all, we generally don't seek medical care when we are feeling well. Medicine is a business. When you run a business, you need customers. When you are sick, you are a customer paying for treatment. **If you have a chronic illness, you may become a customer for a lifetime.**

One of the reasons why you do not hear more about energy medicine and other types of healing modalities is because of the competition with the healthcare industry, not because they are not effective. With alternative therapies, people have had miraculous results that mainstream medicine could not provide, but we do not hear about these testimonials.

It is the censorship of information that has *prevented* preventative medicine.

CHAPTER 22

We Are "Protected" from the "Truth"

You have enemies? Good. That means you've stood up
for something, sometime in your life.
—*Winston Churchill*

When we look at the situation with the cherry farmers, we can see how the FDA is more concerned about protecting us from the truth rather than protecting us from bogus and unsubstantiated claims. It would be one thing if the FDA was going after the individuals and companies that were making fraudulent health claims that were not documented and researched; but *you will see that the people they go after vehemently are the ones who are stating the truth.* These are the people who are under the threat of criminal prosecution. This is why Royal Raymond Rife's work was destroyed. He cured disease using only energy. He was considered a threat.

There are people who are attempting to speak out against the misinformation we are being given from our government agencies. These people are very courageous, knowing full well that a smear campaign may follow to denigrate their reputation as a way to discredit their truthful statements. Dr. David Graham is one of those brave individuals who decided it's time we knew the truth.

David Graham and the FDA

Dr. David Graham was the whistleblower that testified before the Senate Finance Committee against his boss to remove the popular anti-inflammatory drug Vioxx, made by the pharmaceutical giant Merck, from the market. Who was his employer? The FDA.

At the time when Dr. Graham presented his research that detailed the increase in heart attacks and deaths with Vioxx, his supervisors at the FDA retaliated against him and initiated a smear campaign to defame his character and destroy his credentials as a scientist. On August 24, 2004, Dr. Graham presented an abstract at a medical meeting in France; it was an analysis from a Kaiser Permanente database of 1.4 million patients treated with Vioxx, Celebrex, and other NSAIDS (non-steroidal anti-inflammatory drugs). His findings showed that Vioxx was the cause of heart attack or sudden cardiac death in nearly 28,000 patients.[25] Dr. Graham stated to the Senate Committee investigators that the FDA was trying to prevent him from presenting this research.[26]

Merck certainly was no saint in this debacle, either. They unleashed their sales force with aggressive marketing materials to "spin" the data and focus on the reduced digestive tract problems with Vioxx versus other NSAIDS on the market. Merck was aware of the increase in cardiac events in the VIGOR (**Vi**oxx **G**astrointestinal **O**utcomes **R**esearch) study. This study enrolled more than 8,000 participants with rheumatoid arthritis to determine whether Vioxx is better tolerated on the digestive tract than an older pain reliever (naproxen) that has been on the market for years.[27] Naproxen, sold under the trade name, Aleve, has been available as an over-the-counter (OTC) drug available at pharmacies without a prescription since 1994.

The 12-month VIGOR study showed there was a four-fold increased risk of heart attacks with Vioxx compared to naproxen. In this study, naproxen was shown to reduce the incidence of heart attacks and strokes. These study results were published in March 2000.[28] Merck's sales force was able to spin this data and tell physicians that it wasn't that Vioxx had an increase of cardiac events, it just appeared that way when compared to naproxen, which showed to have a cardioprotective effect that reduced heart attacks and strokes. This "interpretation" of the data was basically a hypothesis that was used to counter any culpability for Vioxx. The FDA approved Vioxx, a non-steroidal anti-inflammatory drug (NSAID), on May 20th, 1999, as a pain medication to treat symptoms of osteoarthritis and acute pain.[29] Merck claimed that their studies showed that Vioxx was similar to ibuprofen, but was associated with a reduced incidence of gastrointestinal bleeding.

During this time, Dr. Graham worked for the FDA in the Office of Drug Safety as the associate director for science. He exposed this conflict of interest of the FDA in protecting the drug company in lieu of protecting the American people.

In an interview with Dr. Graham in 2005 on the television program NOW on PBS, he stated, "A former manager of mine from the Office of Drug Safety told me that industry was our client. And when I said to him, 'No, the public is my client,' he said I was wrong and it was industry. And my response back to him was, 'Industry may be your client, but it will never be my client.'"[30]

The Drug Companies Are Clients of the FDA

The FDA is responsible for regulating the same industry that pays them to approve their drugs. The drug companies pay a fee to the FDA to review their drugs for approval. Do you see a conflict of interest here? In 1992, Congress passed The Prescription Drug User Free Act (PDUFA pronounced 'padoofa').[31] This act was placed into effect because the "drug industry" complained that drugs took too long to review and approve. The long delay could potentially cause the drug companies millions for each month the drug was not yet on the market. The FDA complained that they did not have the staff to review all the drugs in a timely manner, so they decided that if the drug companies would pay a fee, the FDA could hire additional drug reviewers to expedite the approval process when a new drug application (NDA) is filed. The fee paid by a drug company to have the clinical data reviewed after filing an NDA is around two million dollars. The drug company's relationship with the FDA has become a little too cozy for comfort, especially since their fees pay the salaries for the drug review staff.

Even with all the mounting evidence that showed the seriousness of the cardiac issues and tens of thousands of patients dying from cardiac related events, it wasn't the FDA that eventually pulled Vioxx from the market. Most people mistakenly came to the conclusion that the FDA intervened and ended the five-year distribution of the drug. It was Merck who decided to voluntarily withdrawal Vioxx from the market on September 30th, 2004 due to safety concerns.[32]

Merck sponsored a three-year study to determine if Vioxx offered a protective effect from the recurrence of colon polyps in patients. They wanted this indication since the competitor, Celebrex, was shown to lower the risk that colon polyps will grow back. This strategy backfired for Merck, who finally conceded after only 18 months into the study that patients on Vioxx had a higher incidence of heart attacks and strokes.[33]

What finally happened? Merck could no longer make excuses for the cardiovascular problems. The design for this long-term study was different from the previous study of Vioxx compared to naproxen. This study compared Vioxx to a placebo and not a competitor drug in the same NSAID group. Finally, Merck no longer had a scapegoat to use for comparison to rationalize why this new study showed patients taking Vioxx were double the risk of cardiac events versus patients taking no drug at all. The fact that Merck withdrew Vioxx on a volunteer basis was only because the study results of increased heart attacks forced them into a situation *to declare a public proclamation of privately guarded information.*

Their deceptive marketing tactics finally caught up with them. Merck was fined $950 million by the U.S. Justice Department to settle a criminal charge for promoting Vioxx for rheumatoid arthritis, which was considered an "off label" promotion since it was outside their promotional indication. The fine also included the civil settlement for the sales force making false and misleading statements regarding the cardiac safety of the drug.[34]

Vioxx was a blockbuster drug due to Merck's aggressive marketing strategies, bringing in worldwide sales of $2.5 billion in 2003.[35] A class action lawsuit filed by several thousand patients was eventually settled in 2007 for $4.85 billion.[36]

In the 2005 interview, The FDA Exposed: An interview with Dr. David Graham, the Vioxx Whistleblower by Manette Louden

Dr. Graham states:

"The FDA is responsible for 140,000 heart attacks and 60,000 dead Americans. That's as many people as were killed in the Vietnam War. Yet the FDA points the finger at me and says, 'Well this guy's a rat, you can't trust him', but nobody is calling them to account. Congress isn't calling them to account. For the American people, it's dropped off the radar screen. They should be screaming because this could happen again."[37]

If something doesn't make sense— it may be *senseless*.

Evidently, a heart attack is an acceptable "side effect" to the FDA for an approved drug. Even stroke is acceptable. Thousands upon thousands of Americans dying is an acceptable side effect as well. These are the side effects of Vioxx and many other prescription drugs on the market. But claiming a person could have a health benefit from unapproved broccoli, walnuts, cherries, and pomegranates with zero side effects is unacceptable and a crime punishable by law. This is such a travesty that even while writing this I cannot believe the absurdity of it all.

There are countless examples to use for the benefits of healing foods and vitamins and other supplements on the market. I just chose a few of these. For the record, I do not believe that all drug companies are evil monsters. Some people may think it seems like a bizarre dichotomy that I am a healer *and* work for a drug company. I certainly don't see it this way at all. Many of these approved pharmaceuticals are helping people by controlling symptoms, alleviating pain, and prolonging life. Both of these jobs that I do are with the intention to help alleviate suffering, whether it is to educate doctors to help them diagnose their patients to get the appropriate treatment or facilitate a healing session to restore balance and help the person to heal. For me, these two jobs complement each other rather than oppose and conflict with one another.

Again, just like with any other business, there are companies that truly have a desire to do good and others that have a primary focus on making money and increasing their stock price. All companies are in the business to make money. The difference is that some companies operate with the highest intentions to provide a beneficial service, while others advance their intention for greed at all cost.

The real evil is the suppression of information and widespread misinformation that prevents us from making informed choices about our healthcare.

Alternative Therapies Work in Harmony with the Body

Our foods, nutritional supplements, and herbal therapies work to restore a natural balance to our bodies. There is no reason why we should not have the information on various foods and vitamins that could help us make informed choices on what may help us heal. If there is a food that has shown to help slow down a specific disease, shouldn't we be able to have access to this information? If a food has been studied and researched to prevent cancer, would you start eating more of it? How can we make healthy choices when we only have a limited option? The real issue is that we don't even know about other options.

Can you imagine being in the hospital recuperating from a stroke or heart attack and having an energy medicine session, acupuncture, or the Rife technology "beam ray" treatment during your stay to assist in your recovery and reduce your number of days spent in the hospital? While many hospitals now use integrative medicine to help patients heal and to increase their satisfaction, I do believe that in the future we will possibly see alternative therapies used more. This could potentially save insurance companies millions of dollars a year if patients have a faster recovery. I see this as the future of medicine where hospitals will have an Energy Medicine Department that will employ healers to reduce costly medical procedures, medications, and hospital days.

High dose IV (intravenous) vitamin C has shown to be effective in cancer, but we do not hear about this information since it can't be patented because it is natural substance—not something that was invented or created in a laboratory. This therapy would compete with the mega expensive chemotherapy drugs that cost thousands of dollars. Since IV Vitamin C does not have the potential to obtain a patent, drug companies are not interested in funding the clinical trials and marketing the "drug." Are you starting to see a pattern here? There are other options that are available to us, but these options may be inexpensive and may not be profitable for the drug companies. Norman Cousins, in addition to his laughter therapy, also received high dose IV vitamin C to treat his ankylosing spondylitis to help boost his immune function and reduce inflammation.

The Road to Wellness

So now you see, there is more than one path to healing. There are many routes available, but some of these side streets are hidden from view. Healthcare in this country is similar to trying to read a big roadmap. How do you find these off-beaten paths? Sometimes we learn about the way from other people or possibly from our own efforts of seeking and exploring a different approach. The way our medical system is devised today in this country, the conventional allopathic medicine would be considered the main road and other options are off the well-trodden road on different paths. Some of these paths may be well paved and have greater visibility, and we can find these side roads and use them as an alternative route. Other paths are less paved and more difficult to find, while some are completely hidden from view. There are many paths off the main road of conventional healing; we need to keep our hearts and minds open to find them. If you seek your truth, the hidden truths will be revealed to you. Always keep an open heart and an open mind about your healing options.

This Is Your Life

Hopefully, now you have a better understanding and a heightened awareness about the importance of being a partner in your wellness prevention plan and treatment choices. If your caregiver is dogmatic in their approach with, "This is your only option," and does not welcome questions regarding your own care, then you may want to think about changing your current healthcare provider. Do you feel as though you are a *partner* in your treatment plan or do you feel that you are being *persuaded* to do whatever your practitioner tells you to do? This is a big difference. When you have no voice and your concerns are not heard or welcomed, you are giving away all your power to this one individual who believes only this drug or treatment will help you. Make sure you have a voice. This is your body. This is your life.

When someone asks me the reasons why they have never heard of energy medicine and other alternative therapies, including the healing power of vitamins and foods, my answer would be: **All of the above.**

SECTION III

....

LOVE

To love oneself is the beginning of a lifelong romance.
—Oscar Wilde

....

CHAPTER 23

Why Do We Love LOVE?

Keep away from people who try to belittle your ambition. Small
people always do that, but the really great ones make you
feel that you too can become great.

—Mark Twain

Love is the most powerful force in the Universe. Our entire existence is created from this energy. Love is the sustenance of the Universe. You can think of love as a food that feeds everything in actuality. The food that we eat and the water we drink nourish our bodies, but it is love that feeds the soul. The Universe *is* LOVE—the base vibration and building block of every creation. The vibration of universal, unconditional love is the pure essence of humans.

Our pure essence is pure love.

Why is the pure essence of everything the vibration and frequency of love? We came from Love. Love is creation. Love is Source. Love is GOD. We exist from the creation of pure unconditional love. This is why love feels so good. When we feel love, we are invincible. We feel like we can do anything. Love opens doors to new and powerful possibilities. When we feel loved, we can accomplish things we never thought were possible.

With love, we are able to accomplish the impossible, think the unthinkable, imagine the unimagined, and create the most spectacular creations.

Love and light are both energy, but with love; we feel the *emotion* of love. Infinite love is the only thing we take with us from incarnation to incarnation. Throughout time and existence, Love sustains the soul. Love is power. Love is Light. Love is GOD.

The Love energy is the essence of everything. This is the highest vibration. Love is the paradise vibration; the energy from HOME. This is the energy from which we are created. In our purest form, this is our essence: WE ARE LOVE.

Love Alters Our DNA

Since we know that love is the most powerful frequency on the planet, can love change our DNA? Yes! When we love ourselves, our body responds to this emotion. When we love ourselves, our health is better because every cell in our body feels and responds to the frequency of this higher vibration. Love heals the Human. Love heals Nature. Love heals the Planet. When we don't love ourselves, we cannot be balanced. How can we be balanced and healthy when our bodies are constantly being bombarded with the emotion of hate and self-loathing? What if our cells constantly get the message that we hate them? This emotion is energy, and our cells are listening and responding. Because our cells have consciousness, they respond to this vibration at the DNA level. And guess what? The DNA is altered. We know that stress can change our DNA and change the normal vibration of our cells, and so can our internal dialogue of our current emotions whether it might be anger, hatred, and even self-hatred.

As previously discussed, everything in existence has its own signature vibration and thus has a corresponding frequency. The energy of love is the highest vibration and has the highest frequency. The love frequency changes all in existence. *Even the Earth has consciousness and can feel the energy of love.* Humans also respond to love. If love is withheld from babies, they do not grow and develop normally.

Remembering the love of another person, alive or deceased, can give us great willpower and courage to endure the challenges in our life. This is the power of love. Humans, plants, nature, animals, water, and our Earth, are all connected and are able to feel the highest vibration of love on the planet.

When people do not have love in their life, they are more prone to illness and stress. We know that people recover more quickly when surrounded by the people who cherish them. **Love is a very powerful energy, and we know that energy of a higher vibration can heal.** Anita Moorjani had a rapid healing when during her NDE she realized her own magnificence. It was this *shift to self-love* that was a catalyst for her spontaneous remission.

To exist with love is real. Love is the only thing we take with us from incarnation to incarnation. Love fills and nourishes our heart and soul on our Earth journey.

SELF-LOVE

We are so busy trying to express affection to others in our life that we sometimes forget the importance of self-love. *Loving ourselves is our greatest gift.* You can only give more of what you have inside of you to give. *If you do not love yourself, it becomes more difficult to give and accept love from other people.* If you do not feel very good about yourself at a particular time in your life, you may push people away who want to love you and be in your life. Have you ever heard someone say, "I just met the right person at the right time in my life," and they got married or started a committed relationship? The "right time" could have been the right time when you accepted the love from another person. You were in a place in your life when you felt good enough about yourself to welcome this love. *When we do not love ourselves, we tend to attract relationships into our life that are abusive.*

We might think of abuse as physical, but it can be verbal and emotional as well. The abuser may belittle us and constantly say things to chip away at our self-esteem to bring us down to their level. This is abuse. Possibly the other person does not want you to feel good about yourself for fear that you will leave them. The other person may not feel that they are worthy of your love or not good enough to be loved by you.

Even withholding love and affection because you don't want your partner to feel good about themselves and you want them to feel "needy" as opposed to "empowered" is a form of emotional abuse.

Love is powerful and withholding your emotion and love with the intention for the other person to feel more insecure and needy is abuse. If you are in a relationship like this, it is time to have an honest and open conversation with your partner. If the relationship is based on fear—fear of the other person leaving you based on your own insecurities and lack of self-love, the relationship cannot grow and blossom. A healthy relationship is founded on trust and commitment, in a nurturing and supportive way. It is not based on fear. If you think about it, most of us probably talk nicer to our dog than we do to the people in our life we profess to love.

Send Yourself a Love Message

When we love ourselves, we send these messages of love to our bodies. On a cellular level, we change and vibrate with this higher frequency. Loving ourselves supports our immune function since we are giving our bodies messages of love—*self-love.*

If your body is constantly reacting to messages of "I hate myself; I am not good enough; I don't want to live; I hate my life; I am worthless," then your body responds to this internal dialogue. The cells in our body are listening and hearing everything *spoken and unspoken.* We are also sending out this vibration to the Universe, and these messages are now traveling to attract like vibrations. This inner conversation keeps us at a lower vibration and limits all the good things the Universe can bring to us.

Dr. Emoto showed how the vibration of negative words could affect the formation of water crystals. This is because these words carry a real energy. The vibration of these words also causes a change in the vibration of our body because our body takes in information, just like water takes in information. The words *love* and *gratitude* and other positive words formed beautiful crystals because the water received a higher vibration as opposed to the lower vibration/frequency of negative words. When you speak affirmations of love, gratitude, peace, joy, and appreciation to yourself, your cells will respond to this new information. Every cell, organ, and structure in your body will now be more in alignment with the vibration of health and vitality.

Why do we find it easier to love others than to love ourselves? We seem to be more accepting and less critical of other's faults and shortcomings than our own. The measuring stick we use to judge ourselves usually sets us up for failure. We think we need to reach to the top of the stick, somewhere hovering near the perfection line. We don't look at others in our lives and expect them to be perfect. We accept that they are in a state of evolving and learning and will undoubtedly make mistakes and let us down from time to time. We don't expect them to have perfect bodies and movie star good looks. We want people in our lives that will be there for us, understand us, and really listen to what we have to say. We all want to be heard. We are comfortable around individuals that we have fun with and feel an easy, unassuming connection with. But then we look at ourselves in the mirror and expect only perfection to be worthy of love. Others are looking at you and hoping for what you hope for—a good, caring, compassionate, trustworthy friend who will be there to make life more fun and less lonely, to support and listen to you, and to love you.

Love Is Healing

Without love and, just as importantly, self-love, we are more prone to illness and disease. How can the immune cells function optimally when they are listening to constant dialogue of an internal tape player stuck on repeat—of negativity and self-loathing?

Try to get in the habit of looking in the mirror and focusing on the positive. Talk to yourself. Get in the habit of being your #1 cheerleader. There is nothing wrong with you being your biggest fan. You don't have to go around bragging about yourself. Cultivate a quiet confidence and elevated esteem—the realization that you are unique and worthy of love. Focus on all the attributes you like and say them aloud. These affirmations will create a new habit of thinking positively. It sounds simple, but it works because you are creating a new awareness of the importance of loving and healing yourself. This subtle shift in perception will create your new reality shift and force you to be more present in your life and aware of your feelings about YOU. All it takes is this simple shift in awareness—paying attention to this present moment.

You now know the highest vibration on the planet is unconditional love. *Unconditionally love yourself! Accept yourself.* Love yourself and you will raise your consciousness and vibration. Why do you care so much what others think about you? If you surround yourself with people who are not loving, supportive, and uplifting, why in the

world would you want to spend time with these people anyhow???
Spend time with people who you enjoy, feel at ease with, and who
appreciate YOU!

Stop trying so hard to fit in with a group of people that you *don't*
fit in with. This does not mean there is something wrong with you.
It's just that this is not your *frequency group*. Have you ever heard the
phrase "birds of a feather flock together"? This popular saying means
that people tend to associate with others who are like them. *Like-
minded people attract like-minded people.* I have been at jobs where
I felt so out of place and never fit in. I have been in various social
functions and felt awkward and did not fit in as well. It will always be
this way. You won't connect with everyone, so don't force it. Trying
to fit in where you don't fit in is like putting a square peg in a round
hole. It doesn't fit.

CHAPTER 24

Being of Service

Our prime purpose in this life is to help others. And if you can't help them, at least don't hurt them.

—*Dalai Lama*

How Can I Help You?

Do you remember how you felt when you tried to give someone a gift, and it was turned down? It could have even been a small gift or a handmade gift, probably not even something of great value. Even if you do not remember what the gift was, you still remember how you felt when it was waved away as unnecessary or unwanted. Have you ever offered a kind act for someone or volunteered to help when needed and the offer was quickly dismissed? Maybe it was a small gesture like offering to help a single mom pick up her daughter from ballet class since your daughter was in the same class. Your feelings may be a little hurt when a kind act is quickly refused. Sometimes we turn down a gift or act of kindness because we really are too uncomfortable of accepting. We don't know how to graciously accept a gift. We may feel uncomfortable as though we are a burden and putting someone else out.

This is a good exercise in shifting your perception to look at another's point of view. Even if you were uncomfortable accepting any type of assistance in the past, think about how you felt when your offer was rejected. Recall a situation when your gift was refused and what you experienced. You may have felt embarrassed and possibly a little inappropriate. I realize this is not a "one-size-fits-all" type of scenario. Sometimes a gift may not be appropriate to give or receive. I know there are times when an offer of assistance is dismissed because it is not needed or wanted. I am referring to instances that are appropriate and rejected because we do not know how to welcome help when offered. We do not know how to accept a gift for holidays, birthdays, or even a gift of someone showing us gratitude or appreciation for something.

What many people don't realize is that when we accept a gift and offer of assistance, we are giving a gift back to the giver. The "gift" we are giving back is helping to fulfill the desire of the person wanting to do something positive for us. People have a need to help and to perform good deeds. It makes us happy. We are uplifted. We feel good about ourselves when we do nice things. Being of service and feeling needed may fulfill a sense of purpose for some people and even help to relieve their anxiety and depression. You are gifting these wonderful feelings to the giver of the gift. When you accept, this is essentially a *gift exchange.*

We become the *gift receiver* and *gift giver*.

At first, you may feel a little out of your comfort zone, but keep in mind that you are also bestowing a gift back to the other person. By allowing their need to help you, or by graciously accepting their present, you are helping them fulfill a purpose that makes them feel genuine and appreciated. Next time look at the giver in the eyes, smile and say, "Thank you" or "I appreciate that." Graciously accept. If you would like to see how it is done, bring me a gift and I will happily demonstrate. (wink)

It's About Being Valued

Don't we all want to feel appreciated and valued, whether it is from our family, our kids, our friends, or our employer? It is not a good feeling to feel like the things that you do go unnoticed and unrecognized. Many relationships begin to crumble with, "I don't feel appreciated." People leave jobs, and sometimes will even accept another job where the pay is lower because "I don't feel appreciated." *We want to feel valued.*

Have you ever complimented someone and they replied, "You just made my day!"? It may have been something simple like, "You look really nice today." Maybe you complimented the salesperson at a store you frequent, "You always take such good care of me!" You may have a friend who always seems to be there for you and exclaimed, "I really value our friendship!" It really didn't matter exactly what you said to the person, it mattered that you said . . . something. You acknowledged that person. You showed your appreciation for them.

Have the awareness to look those in the eye who provide a service for you and say "thank you." It does not matter what type of work they are doing. Your life is easier and better because of the work that they do. Next time you have your car cleaned, your groceries bagged, your clothes dry cleaned, your trash hauled away, your sweet tea refilled (Yes . . . here in the South we drink our tea sweet.) acknowledge them. You know what will happen? Your service will become better!! That person will feel appreciated and will actually want to provide good service to you. Why? Because people do a better job when they are appreciated. I even tell my boss that I appreciate how he notices and comments on the work that I do. "I feel more motivated," is what I have said to him numerous times. I feel like I am seen as a person and not just as a source of business for the company. I like feeling appreciated, too!!

It has become commonplace to judge people based on the work that they do, their job title, the amount of money they make, the clothes they wear, the car they drive, etc. This has become a habit of our conditioning. No parent says to their kid, "I want you to be a failure when you grow up." We are encouraged to be successful at an early age. "I want you to be successful—have a good job, make a lot of money." This is what kids predominately hear during their childhood, so they grow up with a definition of success: having a good paying job, or a high profile status career such as a doctor or lawyer (This gives parents bragging rights.). This is what is considered as "making a good living."

What Do *You* Consider Success?

I was asked during an interview by the hiring manager for a pharmaceutical sales job, "Do you consider yourself successful and why?" I replied, "I consider myself very successful. I have a wonderful family who loves me, and I love very much, and I am able to do a job that I really enjoy doing." As soon as I was done speaking, I saw the expression of utter confusion and disgust sweep over his face. I knew if he thought he could get away with rolling his eyes—he would have! I also knew that I just blew the interview at that moment. So, I filled in the awkward silence and continued, "I know that you are expecting me to say, 'I am successful because I make a lot of money.'" I paused as his face lit up in his acknowledgement that . . . yes . . . I was now on the right track. "But I don't consider money to be a measure of success," I continued. "I consider these scientists and researchers who discover these drugs to be very successful."

"So do I!" he interjected,

"And yet, we make more money than they do."

"Good point!" he hollered like I just hit the winning shot in a tennis match. He beamed thinking that I had singlehandedly come up with the most revolutionary concept he has ever heard! *Money is not the only measure of success.* I even saw a half smile cross his face. Guess what! I did get the job. I found out a few months after I was hired that he told the recruiter and his boss that I was the smartest person he had ever interviewed! One day when my manager and I were working out in the field making sales calls, I said to him, "Remember during our interview, you asked me if I consider myself successful and why? I felt like I blew the interview and definitely was not going to get the job. I knew you were expecting me say I made a lot of money, and that was success."

"Yeah, I remember I wasn't going to hire you!" he said. "I decided right then that you would not be motivated as a sales rep if you didn't care about making a lot of money. But then I realized you were right—there are people I would consider to be successful who don't get paid as well."

It is unfortunate that you could consider someone as being lesser than you based on what job they do, how much money they make, how good looking they are, how big their house is, and the status of their job. By doing this, you are silently stating, *I am superior to you.* I am superior because I have more money. I am superior because I am better looking than you. I am superior because my job title has more status than yours.

We silently scrutinize the people that we meet as they silently scrutinize us. It's funny when you think about it because we pretend that the other person does not know we are doing this. They know! They are doing the same thing back to you!

We are all souls evolving and learning life lessons based on our own soul path. This is why it is so important not to judge. People are constantly doing different jobs. I have had several different jobs since college, some were really crappy, in my opinion, and some were great. I have still been the same person all along. People should not be treated differently because someone has a high status job or makes more money than you. Do you see how ridiculous this is once you realize we are all on our own path?

The person who is waiting tables may become the CEO of a million dollar company next year—you don't know. Not everyone has the same interests. This is a good thing! If everyone wanted to be a doctor or lawyer, then we would have few people in other areas of service. Who would we have to be cooks, accountants, builders, and the many other jobs we depend on? If you asked ten different people what their definition of success is, you will get ten different answers because success depends on what *you* measure success to be. For you, money may be what you consider to be the achievement of success. Someone else may consider success to be—just being happy in life. Success for another person could be taking care of the kids and making sure everything with the house runs smoothly. Success could be a person who tries to see the good in everyone and strives to be a better person every day. Success could be just making it through the day!

Look at it this way: if your only benchmark for success is money and if a person won the lottery, would you suddenly consider that person a huge success because now they have millions? Why do we hoard our money and material possessions while we are alive? We can't take it with us. We take the love with us when we leave this incarnation. We don't have a bank account on the other side. We don't have stock options and mutual funds and a retirement plan. There is enough money in the world so that everyone has food, shelter, and clean water, the basic needs for survival.

The problems that we have in the world are the problems we created and the problems we do have the resources to resolve.

There is certainly nothing wrong with wanting money to have the things that we want and have a fun, comfortable, enjoyable life. However, it's unjustified judging someone based on their income level and their material possessions, or even physical attractiveness.

As we get older and have more life experience and greater awareness of what truly is important to us, our definition of success will shift because we are constantly changing. If someone asked me today in an interview, "Do you consider yourself successful and why," what would I say?

"I consider myself successful because I strive to increase planetary consciousness by being a catalyst to help awaken people to who they really are." Do you think I would get the job?! Ha! Hopefully, this book will be published, and I won't have to interview for another drug rep job again.

CHAPTER 25

The LIGHT Is LOVE

Darkness cannot drive out darkness; only light can do that. Hate cannot drive out hate; only love can do that.

—Martin Luther King, Jr.

In the Bible, God said **Let there be light:** and there was light. Everything is composed of light. Light is Intelligent. Light is Information. Light is Love. Light is Energy. Light is Consciousness. Light is God. When we think of light, we think of the absence of dark.

Light is conscious energy. The entire Universe is composed of light, and this conscious energy exists in all the spaces of the Universe, even in the void.

There is something always present in that void—consciousness.

Everything in existence is actually vibrating particles of LIGHT. We live in a Universe of living light. Think about it this way:

Light is Energy. Energy is Matter. *Light is Energy and Matter.*

Light is Everywhere. We may only think of light as the anticipated daily event of the darkness of night being dispelled as the early dawn comes every morning and awakens us from our slumber. Light can be seen. We see it passing through the branches of a tree when we just sit and relax for some shade during the day. I love watching the beams of light dance in their own joy through the branches of trees when I take a walk through a wooded area to enjoy time in nature. We see the light reflected in our hair as it glistens and shines. We see the light when we look into another person's eyes as the color sparkles. We see the light coming through the window replacing darkness in a room. Have you ever washed your car and stood there admiring the way the light hits the chrome and blinds you in its reflection? And have you felt proud and delighted with the freshly washed, dirt-free, radiant color shining brilliantly? We see the beautiful colorful light in a rainbow above in the sky after it rains. A photographer will look through the camera lens to take the perfect picture, utilizing the illumination of the light to capture the magnificent, natural beauty of the intended object being photographed.

Light is in everything in existence. And we are connected through strands of light. Although I do not see this light that links all things at all times, I perceive it. I sense this interconnection of light altering the vibration and frequency of everything everywhere. By saying we are all "connected" is describing a relationship with everything in existence, as if we have an attachment to another object, event, or situation. A more accurate way of viewing our connection to everything as strands and particles of light is to say that we are *interconnected.*

When we are "interconnected" with something, we are connected in a way that one aspect of something affects the relationship with an aspect of another.

We are interconnected because every vibration of our being affects the vibration of everything in existence. This is how light changes the frequency and vibration of everything it comes into contact with. Light is the interconnection of all things, which means that when one person raises their vibration, we are all affected because our vibration is raised as well. It has to be. This is why it is so important to focus on raising our own individual vibration to bring more light onto the planet. When we do so, we are bringing these things associated with a lighter and higher vibration such as love, peace, joy, compassion, information, and truth.

We have the power to create a planet of peace right now on Earth if we want to. There are seven billion people on the planet. Can you imagine if we could harness more light onto the planet just by consciously being mindful of living in a higher vibration of love, gratitude, and peace? We could create a virtual paradise here. Even if only one percent of the people, that is seventy million, focused on bringing additional light onto the planet we would have a completely different world. Could you imagine living on Earth with no war, poverty, hunger, illness, and control of the people through fear tactics and terror? This can happen, and it *is* happening.

The Shift

Years ago, there were many new age books talking about "The Shift." This is the shift, right here, right now: the shift in awareness, in consciousness, in our current way of thinking. The "shift" is a spiritual awakening across the planet. We are moving toward a direction (shifting) to create a planet with an existence filled with peace, joy, love, and truthful information. This is LIGHT. This is what it means to bring light onto the planet. Light displaces Darkness. What is Darkness? It is the absence of everything associated with light. This is the absence of knowledge, joy, happiness, peace, and love. Darkness is greed, fear, violence, hatred, and destruction. It is also the deceit and intentional misinformation we have on the planet to try to keep us in a state of perpetual fear and oppression. This is the meaning of the phrase "kept in the dark." When we are kept in the dark, we do not have information. Light is information. We become enlightened when we are informed.

When we have clarity about something, we use the expression "see the light." We are created from light and are one with it. All of us are extensions of this source energy, which is light. We are all a part of everything, and everything is a part of us. How can we be separate from Source and from each other if we are from the same origin? We can't. It's like making a big batch of chocolate chip cookies, and you place twenty cookies on the cookie sheet. They appear to be separate individualized cookies, but they are all from the same batch. Even if you gave these cookies to twenty different people to be eaten individually and the cookies appear to be separate, they were all made from the same cookie batter. We play this game of being separate so that we can experience life, make choices with our free will, and remember that we are one with our Creator as spiritual beings.

Each one of us is a divine spark of light from this source energy of God. How can we be separate from God when we are created from the energy of God? We are not and cannot be separate . . . EVER. We are each an individualized expression of this God Force energy. **I am distinctly me; you are distinctly you,** even though we are created from the same source energy.

We are all beings of light. We are spiritual beings of light.

I See the Light

When someone has had a near-death experience (NDE) and recounted what happened, it has been close to universal that the experience involved seeing and/or feeling the presence of a bright light. *I saw the brightest light I have ever seen. I felt the most unconditional love I have ever experienced. It was a pure bliss. I felt myself moving toward the light. I had a sense of knowing that I had not experienced before as if I was now "awake."* These are typical comments from people who have either clinically died or were close to death.

What is this LIGHT? **This Light is YOU.** This bright white light of pure unconditional love, peace, joy, knowledge, and pure bliss is you. This is our essence of who we are. We are the light of pure love. This is our God Force energy. We are from this light, and we feel at "home" when we go back to this light.

We are from the realm of light.

One day, we will return to the realm of light: our home between incarnations. We are a vessel of light energy as spiritual beings. The sense of knowing that we are from this love is wired into our DNA. This "knowing" is in our cell memory, and because of this during our lifetime, we long to find a purpose to our life. We long to find our connection with our God Force energy. This is what we may refer to as a "reconnection" back to our source energy. *This is what religions are based upon, to assist us in our path to understand our connection to God.*

I have mentioned in section I that energy healing reconnects one back to their source energy in raising our vibration and awareness. The word "reconnection" is appropriate since we are essentially connecting back to this energy with our awareness and remembrance of our origin as spiritual beings. For me personally, since I always sense this, I prefer the term "realignment" because it is a matter of aligning ourselves with this source energy that is already present. I was always confused with the term "reconnection." I felt—how could I be reconnected to something I am already connected to? If the connection is there, it is there . . . right? In a spiritual sense, this is true. Our spiritual bodies are composed of this pure light, and those who have had an NDE may have experienced the bliss of this light of unconditional love.

During our death experience, we shed our physical bodies, and we are pure light. We are spiritual beings of light as we leave this physical realm and go back to our spiritual home in "the other realm" or in "heaven" or "back home," whatever term you feel comfortable with. When we are in our physical bodies in this realm, we are playing a game of forgetting that we are a divine spark of this spiritual light of God. So reconnecting back to this source energy is assisting us in our awakening to the oneness of all that is.

Healing with Light

During a session, I am channeling energy in waves of light, which we have been talking about in this chapter. This light is love. This light is energy. *This light is intelligent and works with the higher self of the individual to assist for the appropriate healing to take place.* I am essentially bombarding you with light. Your body is reconnecting with a higher vibrational frequency of light, and every cell will attune to this higher vibration of energy that is introduced during the healing session. When I place my attention on healing an individual, I am creating waves of light. I actually feel waves of light passing through my entire body and even more forcefully through my hands.

Are YOU Working in the Light?

When we are trying to make a positive difference in the world with intent to help our fellow human, we are working in the light and the Universe supports our endeavors. When we use our gifts to make a positive change, to inspire others to make a difference, to change the human condition for the better, with love in our heart and a motive to truly help, the Universe supports this vibration. When we "work in the light" we attract a "like vibration" in the Universe, which increases our vibration. This cycle continues and builds momentum for our cause, and our gifts that we utilize become stronger since supported by the light.

Conversely, if we use our gifts for greed, corruption, and power, they will have a lower vibrational frequency and attract similar lower frequencies that are not of the light, perpetuating more greed and corruption. This is why we are striving to bring light onto the planet. As you recall, light dispels the darkness. By all of us working together to bring more light onto the planet, the darkness and lower vibrational energy of greed, corruption, violence, and the suppression of truthful information will disintegrate and begin to crumble. It must because it will not be sustained on a planet of a higher vibration.

We are purposefully harnessing additional light in order to eliminate the darkness on Earth. The darkness of evil, greed, hatred, genocide, war, and misinformation will cease to exist because it will not be supported by the light nor supported on a planet with a higher vibration of love. "Lightworkers" are people who *work to bring light* onto the planet. How do you become a Lightworker? By working in the light to create a positive change in the world. Living your life to raise your vibration to assist in creating peace on Earth. Being aware that your words, thoughts, emotions, and actions are part of the *global mind* that affects all things because we are all interconnected. Does this sound like you?? Welcome aboard! We need you, Lightworker!!

Even you, who are reading this book, are bringing more light onto the planet by raising your awareness and increasing your vibration. How can you bring more light onto the planet? You can have the intent of creating a planet of love and peace, and not focusing on the evening news and national headlines, which propel the masses into a constantly high state of fear and anxiety.

FEAR does not contribute to the light of the planet. Fear and anxiety lower our vibration and this, in turn, lowers the collective vibration of humanity. When we are afraid, we are much more willing to give our power away under the guise of "protection."

Fear serves a purpose for those who want to control others. The purpose is to gain power in return for a *perceived sense of security*. We are more inclined to give up our individual rights for greater government control when we are told, "It's for our own protection." Finally, the time comes when we realize we have very little freedom left because we were afraid and voluntarily gave up our human rights in return for a promise of greater security and protection from harm. Think this can't happen? This already is happening.

We do have the power to create the world that we want to live in. Very soon the emotions and actions that are not congruent with love—such as greed, rage, violence and war—will not be supported by the Universe and will no longer be sustained. Businesses that are run by greed and corruption, with a need to dominate, will collapse. Services and companies that support people and cater to benefit humanity will thrive and be successful. This will be the new planet EARTH. We are on our way, working toward creating a New Earth in this lifetime. How are we going to do this? We will do this by increasing our God-given light on the planet and "Living our Light." After all: **We are the light of God manifest in form.**

CHAPTER 26

Life Is funny!

I'm not offended by all the dumb blonde jokes because I know I'm not dumb . . . and I also know that I'm not blonde.

—*Dolly Parton*

I know for a fact there is laughter in heaven. If there were no laughter, it would not be heaven! That's how I know. People love to laugh!! I wrote a book—*It's Just MY Nonsense*—that has been available for several years. As you can infer from the title, it's a comedy. It may seem a little unusual to some that I also enjoy writing comedy. I am a goofball, silly, and love to laugh. And with that being said, I can also be a spiritual person who has always had a desire to make a difference in the world. All I ever wanted to do was to change the world, to find a way to make the world a better place by using my gifts and talents to create a planet where we can all get along and play nice. Is that too much to strive for?

My Nonsense book, as I refer to it, is an invitation to the reader to participate in my reality. By writing this stuff down, it is now in a form where you and others can participate in as well. When you read my book, you get to come along and enjoy the ride, to be able to experience how I view life through my eyes. I like to think of my writing as my calling card to the Universe: *This is how I see the world. This is my reality!!* The things people do and say are funny, ridiculous, and even absurd at times. If you don't think people are funny, spend a few moments and think about the people that you know. Think about your comical parents, your eccentric brother or sister, your crazy kids, your weird cousins, your outlandish friends, your annoying neighbors, your boss you suck-up to, your conniving co-workers. I bet when you start thinking about some of these characters in your life, you will start to chuckle because you know people are funny and do funny things. This is what I enjoy writing about: the absurdity in everyday life.

We Remember Funny Things

When there is a funny situation, we remember it! Have you ever had a teacher who incorporated humor into their classroom? Not only did it make the class more enjoyable and helped you to pay attention, you probably remembered more of what you learned. We remember situations and experiences that we think are funny. If I were to ask you about a situation where you laughed so hard you could hardly remain seated in you chair, you would remember it. We have all had a situation that we did not think was funny at the time it occurred; then a bit later when we thought about it, we laughed. "It wasn't funny at the time" is how we have all started a story when talking about something that happened. So, what changed about the situation? Our perspective changed, that's all. After some time, when we reflected on what had happened we saw the situation a little differently. We no longer have the emotional attachment after we are removed from the situation, so we may have this *hilarious hindsight*.

> *"Laughter is an instant vacation."*
> —*Milton Berle*

I love this quote by comedian Milton Berle because when we laugh, we do forget about our problems, even in the briefest of moments. It really is like we are on a quickie vacation. When we laugh, we are focused on the present. In that moment we are happy; we have joy; we are smiling. Laughter is also a pain reducer. When we laugh our body releases its own natural pain relievers such as endorphins, our body's very own morphine. Already sounds like the start of a good vacation . . . huh?

Laughter Is the Best Medicine

Laughter may benefit our heart as well. A study was completed at the University of Maryland where 20 study participants watched 15 minutes of either a stressful movie (opening scene of *Saving Private Ryan*) or a funny movie (segment of *Kingpin*). Blood flow increased during laughter and decreased while watching the stressful segment. Dr. Miller, the director of preventative Cardiology at the University of Maryland Medical Center, was the principal investigator of the study. "The idea to study positive emotions, such as laughter came about after studies had shown that mental stress caused blood vessels to constrict."[38]

In a previous study by Dr. Miller, three hundred participants filled out a questionnaire and rated situations about everyday events on a scale from one to five (not funny to very funny). Of the three hundred volunteers who participated, half of them had a heart attack or coronary artery bypass surgery and the other half did not have heart disease. The heart disease group showed that they exhibited less humor toward everyday situations than the other half without heart disease. "The magnitude of change we saw in the endothelium after laughing was consistent and similar to the benefit we might see with aerobic exercise or statin use," says Dr. Miller.[39]

Watching a funny movie or our favorite sitcom, going to a comedy club and making laughing more of a priority during your day can be heart healthy. Laughter helps the blood vessels dilate so more blood and oxygen can flow to our tissues and organs. Laughter will keep our blood vessels relaxed, becoming more elastic and less rigid. This is what exercise does, what a statin drug does, and we can accomplish this just by living a life filled with laughter.

Did you know that the highest incidence of heart attacks occurs on Monday mornings? This is due to the "back to work blues" Stress affects our health. The start of the workweek is very stressful. We all look forward to the weekend, which may be why there was a decrease in heart attacks by the end of the week. The saying "I live for my weekends" may hold some truth. It was interesting to note that if Monday landed on a national holiday, the incidence of heart attacks was less on that day.

We may refer to people we know who have an easy laugh and don't take themselves too seriously as "light-hearted." Conversely, we are "heavy-hearted" when we are sad and depressed. People who have experienced the loss of a loved one or had a loving relationship end may feel heartbroken or have a "broken heart." You can have a broken heart from losing anything you love, whether it be the end of a business venture that you loved, a financial ruin, a divorce, or the loss of a beloved pet. This is not imaginary. The heart and all cells respond to our emotions. A broken heart is real. People, as well as animals, have suffered and died from the emotional impact of a broken heart. Our heart does respond to our emotions, and this can change the structure and function of our physical heart. This is not just anecdotal information and speculative; there is much research that supports a link to our emotional health and our physical symptoms. Our bodies and our emotions and our spiritual outlook are all connected. This is what I refer to as the **trinity of wholeness** or the **triad of health**.

A harmonious oneness of body, mind, and spirit.

> ***"Laughter is inner jogging."***
> —*Norman Cousins*

In his book *Anatomy of an Illness*, Norman Cousins stated that laughter helped him to overcome a crippling and degenerative disease that was destroying his connective tissue in his spine. Norman was diagnosed with ankylosing spondylitis, which caused severe inflammation, as his connective tissue was continually being broken down and slowly disintegrating. Norman was in a great deal of pain and had difficulty even moving his limbs. He made the decision to go off all pain medications and give laughter a try. The nurse set up the movie-projector for him in his hospital room so he could watch episodes of the classic television show *Candid Camera* and some old *Marx Brothers films*. Norman discovered that ten minutes of genuine belly laughter acted as an anesthetic, which allowed him to sleep for two hours pain-free. When the pain returned, the movie-projector was turned on again for another laughter episode.[40]

The only side effect from the laughter: he was disturbing the other patients with his boisterous laughter! Norman was able to move out of the hospital and finish his recovery in a more accommodating and comfortable environment: a hotel room! When the specialists had first explained to Norman that his disease was incurable, he didn't accept this as a reality; and because of this, he did not fear having an "incurable" illness.[41]

Do We Have to Learn How to Laugh Again?

Have we forgotten how to laugh? It's as though by the time we reach adulthood, we have been told not to laugh so much and "act like a grown-up" and not be silly. We have forgotten how easy it was to laugh. We go to laughing clubs and yoga laughing classes so we can practice how to laugh. What the heck happened to us? We now join clubs and take classes to teach us how to laugh and practice laughing with the other people who do not remember how to laugh. What's next? Are we going to have potty training clubs and farting clubs to teach us how to reclaim our basic human functions? What kind of a society do we live in that we have to learn to laugh and practice "fake laughing" so that our body will have the physical benefits of laughter?

Do babies "fake laugh"? Babies do not need to learn to laugh. They just laugh easily and naturally. As adults, we have associated an easy laugh with immaturity and a lack of professionalism in the workplace. Some people think if you laugh you don't care about anything, or you're not serious enough. I think these clubs help us to get back in the habit of laughing again because we have created a habit of not laughing. It's as though we now need to condition the mind and re-train ourselves how to laugh. We have been programmed with responsibility and stress, to take life more seriously: *to act like a grown-up*!

What is missing in a fake laugh is the emotion of pure joy and true happiness. I believe the body does respond by lowering the blood pressure and causing more oxygen to flow. But you know what? There is nothing like a real good, hearty, deep belly laugh from something that is hysterically funny or a gleeful laugh because you are happy! This is a real laugh. A genuine laugh has the emotional and spiritual benefit of releasing negative emotions like anger and sadness, and it is a wonderful stress reducer. As Norman said, "Laughter is internal jogging." Our insides are getting a workout. I prefer to say, "Laughter is *exercise of our innards*." (Just made that up! Haha. . . .) I am certainly not afraid to laugh at myself. I might as well laugh at me before other people do! Why do we take ourselves so seriously? Life should be enjoyable and amusing. All you have to do is find the humor in your own life: *your Nonsense!*

We could do a "fake it" until it's real kind of laugh, but I still believe that laughter as a natural response to genuine humor and joy has the truest benefit, not just physical, but mental and spiritual as well. What is missing is the euphoric feeling we get from a real laugh. Have you ever laughed so hard you felt like you needed a nap? This is the "lightness" you get from an authentic laugh that's associated with a reduction of stress and anxiety. After all, Norman Cousins did not heal himself with fake laughter; he healed himself watching movies and TV shows that were hilarious and made him really laugh.

If you are sad, depressed, and miserable, a fake laugh is not going to change your outlook into a joyful mood. You may start to feel a little silly trying to force yourself to feel a certain emotion like joy when you are not "feeling it." It's those funny little things in everyday life that cause babies to laugh before they are able to speak. A baby's laughter is real, spontaneous, and accompanied with a squeal of sheer delight. Grown-ups know this. Isn't this why we use baby talk, coo, and make silly faces and go to exhausting, embarrassing extremes to get a baby to smile at us and laugh? *I have never seen any baby do laughter yoga!*

Everyone Speaks Laughter

Laughter is the same language for everyone. If you speak Chinese, you still speak laughter. If you speak Spanish, you still speak laughter. We laugh the same in English, too! Laughter is a universal language that we all understand.

Laughter is a catalyst for peace; when we are laughing, we can't be fighting.

Lighten Up

What can we do right now for our health and happiness? *Lighten Up!* Have you even taken a comment too seriously and your friend said, "Lighten up." When we laugh, we release negativity such as stress, depression, and anxiety; the heaviness of these negative, low vibration emotions, are gone in the moment. When our vibration is higher, we feel *lighter*. The high frequency energy of laughter from love and happiness raises the vibration on the planet and increases the light on Earth. Why should we laugh more? Laughter is good for us! It can boost our immunity, release our body's natural pain medication (endorphins), be heart healthy, and make life a bunch more fun! Did you know when we laugh since we raise our vibration and light, we attract more of what we want in life? Joy attracts more experiences into our life to be joyful for. We can heal ourselves and the planet through our natural expression of joyous, jubilant laughter.

You're Still a Kid at Heart

Grown-ups are just older and taller kids. You may have a little more money in your pocket than you did when you were five, but deep down in your heart, you are still that silly, goofy, funny kid who knew how to LAUGH and find happiness in life's little moments! Go find that little kid again!

> *"My grandmother started walking five miles a day when she was sixty. She's ninety-seven now, and we don't know where the hell she is."*
> —*Ellen DeGeneres*

See . . . I knew you remembered how to laugh!

CHAPTER 27

NEW AGE Is the LOVE AGE

There never was a good war or bad peace.
—*Benjamin Franklin*

I f we did not have love on the planet, this Earth would be a very dark place. We would have corporate and political power mongering, war, terror, lack of compassion, poverty, sickness, and a lack of reverence for life. You may be thinking, *we have all this right now in the world.* This is true; we do. The way to reverse all of this is through love. Through love, we will have a more fair and equitable distribution of wealth. We would find a way to end conflict peacefully without war. We would have compassion and make sure everyone who desires food, shelter and clean water has this. There would not be the hording of wealth in banks, stock markets, and corporations. Money would be used to help those in need. Jealousy would not be a problem because abundance could be available to anyone as there would be more of an equitable division of wealth.

One day:
- *Love* will replace *Fear*.
- *Knowledge* will replace *Ignorance*.
- *Understanding* will replace *Intolerance*.

Many of us may have already forgotten the doomsday prophesy of the end of the world on December 21, 2012. This predicted "end" was based on the Mayan calendar, which ended after a 26,000-year cycle. The Mayan calendar ended, and you are here and alive reading this book. We are still here, aren't we? This foretelling of doom created quite a bit of fear around the globe. How many of you out there were cramming in the things on your bucket list? What about the people who went on shopping sprees or emptied their savings to live it up before the end-of-the-world? Ouch! That must have hurt when you opened your eyes the next morning and realized the bill is on its way!

I like to think of the prophesy as the end of the old world and a beginning of the new world. *An end of something creates a beginning for something else*—a new beginning of a commitment to continue to raise the vibration of the planet toward the higher vibration of love. For those of you who do not think we are raising the vibration on the planet, look at all the children who have been born in the last decade. They are much different than we are. They are not just more advanced because they were born during the "technology age" and played with all these cool gadgets since birth. They are more aware than we were at their same age, and because of this, most of them probably think this planet is insane.

Look at your own kids; see how different they are than you were as a kid. These "new kids" are born at a higher vibration because the planet is at a higher vibration than it was when we were born. These incoming souls are at a higher vibration at birth. They are smart, more planet conscious, and have the awareness to *want* to live in a more peaceful world.

Anti-War vs. Pro-Peace

Mother Teresa once said: "I will never attend an anti-war rally; if you have a peace rally, invite me."

Mother Teresa understood that supporting an anti-war rally is still focusing on war. She knew that there was power in numbers, and a huge crowd rallying around war only creates more thoughts about war. When hundreds of people are chanting, "I don't want WAR!" the Universe responds: And so it is! *Keep not wanting war.* This does not bring peace. The energy of the rally actually supports war. The Universe does not hear "I am against war, and I want to stop war." The Universe forms energy on what we focus on: WAR. A peace rally is focusing on PEACE. A crowd of people with a focus of **"I want PEACE"** is very different than a mass focus of **"I don't want WAR."** If we do not want war, than why focus our time and energy on war?

Attending an anti-war rally, our thoughts and actions are about war, our posters are about war, and we talk about war. This is quite a bit different than a pro-peace rally about peace. Do you see the difference? In a pro-peace rally, our thoughts and actions and feelings are about peace. *An anti-war rally is not a pro-peace rally.* Anti-war is not creating peace. It would be like attending an anti-hate rally vs. attending a LOVE rally. One is creating the energy around hate, while the other is creating the energy around love.

War Is Barbaric

One day we will have the awareness to see clearly the calamity of war with a new perspective. We will see WAR as an act of vacuous barbarism of self-destruction with extreme planetary consequences affecting Mother Earth and everything in existence.

War is created in the minds of humans. This is where wars start. We decide to kill based on our own greed for power, money, and control over each other. It does not matter what the reason is—it could be no reason at all, for that matter. Everything about war is barbaric.

WAR is a barbaric human *miscreation.*

War is the insanity of humankind. It is the *Kill* or *Be Killed* mentality. War creates destruction, fear, homelessness, and hunger; it destroys lives and creates poverty. We spend billions of dollars to fund a war. This money could be used to help so many people. Just think if all the money used to fund war was used so that every single person on the planet had shelter, food, clean water, and medical care. This is a possibility; there is enough for everyone. We put our resources toward war and destruction. That is a choice.

We could choose to allocate monies to accentuate life not accelerate death.

We do have a choice. There are always options. The companies that make military equipment, aircraft, guns, missiles, tanks, etc. have multi-million dollar contracts. The suppliers for electronics and communication systems for the military also make billions of dollars. There is a lot of money to be made from war.

A recent 2013 report from Brown University, referred to as the *Costs of War Project,* showed the US spending for the Iraq war at $6 trillion. This amount not only includes the direct costs of war, but also the indirect costs such as interest owed on the debt, caring for the wounded veterans, medical and disability claims for the veterans.[42] Do you think $6 trillion could change the world? If we could learn to overcome conflict with peaceful solutions, we could eradicate hunger and poverty, create access to housing and clean water, and provide medical care to all people. There are enough resources in the world to make this happen. We *choose* war.

The Unawakened HUMAN Is Destructive

Hitler started the hatred in Germany of the Jews with the power of the word. Six million Jews were killed during the Holocaust in WW2. Hitler spread propaganda about the Jews to perpetuate lies and create the motive for massive hatred. The power of the word traveled far and wide across Germany as lies about the Jews were printed on the front page of the newspapers, in the children's school books, at rallies, on posters, and propaganda was circulated by the distribution of pamphlets.

Why did Hitler hate the Jews? Did Hitler blame the Jews for Germany's defeat in WW1? Did Hitler despise the Jews because they were successful and prominent figures in banking and business, while most of Germany was in an economic crisis? Did Hitler want to create a "superior" Aryan nation of blond-haired, blue-eyed Germans for a "master race" and thus needed to wipe out the "Jewish race" as an ethnic cleansing? All of these reasons are speculative and possible explanations.

How can one truly understand the mind of such monstrous evil? Hitler could have said anything about anyone to create a distorted perception of hatred, but Hitler's focus was mainly on the Jews. Now, the people of Nazi Germany will see the Jews through Hitler's eyes. *The eyes of lies.* The eyes with a master plan of creating a persuasive deception to wipe out an entire race of people that Hitler hated and despised. This is the power of the word. The German Nazi's justified their gruesome and heinous actions based on these lies.

> **"To see and listen to the wicked is already**
> **the beginning of wickedness."**
> **—Confucius**

Hatred can have a way of creating unity amongst people very quickly. Suddenly, a common enemy is created to justify the actions of torture and annihilation. This is how genocide works to abolish any race. War, in general, is annihilation. The goal is to kill the enemy. One day we will all see the barbarism behind war. It's as if we are still cavemen fighting and killing for survival. As long as we have WAR in our world, we will not evolve to enlightened beings. How can we? To **evol**ve comes from **LOVE**. This is why the base of the word *evol*ve is love. Enlightened beings resolve conflict with peaceful solutions. We still have a "last man standing" mentality. We think we as humans are so evolved because we have technology. We use this technology to kill. Does this sound like an evolved species to you?

ONE Person Can Change History

Do you think one person has the power to change the world? Look at the difference one person can make in our lifetime— in our history. One person, such as Hitler, has the power to do great evil. One person also has the power to create change with love and compassion. Look at Mother Theresa. Mother Theresa taught the world about compassion and unconditional love. Each of us has tremendous power to create change in the world. Never underestimate your power. One person does make a difference. By changing ourselves everyday, we change the world. If you think you have to do something on a global scale to create change in our world, you are mistaken. You do not have to be a famous actor, painter, author, scientist, or even Steve Jobs. You don't have to be a brilliant inventor like Thomas Edison. All you need to do is focus on being the best person you can be, to be aware of your vibration, of your thoughts and feelings, and to increase the frequency on the planet. *Become the best YOU and you add to the light of the entire planet.* If seven billion people added to the light in a conscious way, we would have global peace creating a virtual paradise on planet Earth.

Are We Really That Different?

Our entire existence of the human population has been based upon a focus of our differences. How different we are! We have different skin color, different religions to celebrate our Creator, different customs, and different languages. Where has this thought process gotten us? We have spent thousands of years focusing on what separates us. We separate ourselves with our limited thinking.

We create judgments about people based on our own views of what people should look like and what people should believe.

These judgments are created by our individualized biased and prejudiced standards that we live with.

Viewing humans as separate from each other is not from a high vibration of love and peace. This separation has created a low vibration of isolation and fear, which is the cause of war. We create war because we think we are separate from each other. This feeling of isolation creates fear and causes us to be destructive. If we truly understood the energetic connection to each other and that **we are the energy of God manifest in form,** we would not destroy each other. We would not kill each other. There would be a reverence for life. All life. This includes an appreciation and love for Mother Earth. We would have a knowing and understanding that by harming one person we are creating a ripple effect that causes ill effects for everyone.

Reverence for Life

The reason why we have war, genocide and abuse (people and animals) is because we do not have reverence for life. *Reverence for life comes from the vibration of love.* When we have love in our hearts, we cannot imagine harming another. When we observe people doing harm to others, and we do not act or we do not question, we are actually creating more negativity.

Our Silence to the Act Is Our Consent

We are consenting to and assisting in creating a world perpetuated in fear, violence, and negativity through our silence. We promulgate this thought form through our inaction. Silence and inaction is the opposite of love; it is fear. We are creating a world based on the vibration of fear. The adage "Silence is Golden" does not apply here. "Be quiet" applies when we are in a movie theater after the previews have finished and the main attraction is coming on. It does not apply while we are stripped of our power and our human rights and dignity. It takes great courage to speak up and to act when an event is taking place. It takes great courage to stand up and do the right thing. It is time we all found our courage to take action.

When we stand in silence to acts of evil, we are the silent consenters to acts of evil.

War Is the Insanity of Humankind

As long as we have war and genocide on this planet, we are not an evolved species. A species that is evolved knows there are options to war, but there are many more ways to peace. We are not yet evolved enough to find peaceful solutions to conflict. An evolved species does not kill a race of people for their beliefs. An evolved species does not seek to wipe out an entire population of people because they are different. Only through compassion, tolerance, and understanding will we see all people as equal. One day, we will have the vision to see past skin color, different beliefs, and traditions.

It is a travesty to define ourselves as the "most evolved species" on the planet. If this were true, then the most "evolved" of all existence handles conflict through war?! We are actually the "most pompous species" to think we are, as we mass murder based on race, religion, and beliefs that differ from our own. We are meant to be diverse.

The word **AMERICA** is an anagram for **I AM RACE**. War is murder. When under the guise of war, this carries no prison term.

If we were truly evolved, we would be able to resolve conflict peacefully.

If we valued life, there would be no more war. Humans have lost reverence for human life and for all life forms, for that matter. We do not value the animals that provide us with food. We continue to destroy the planet that provides us with a home. If we continue this destruction, we may all find ourselves homeless.

An evolved species understands the interconnectedness of all things and will consciously exist symbiotically with all life forms for a peaceful cohabitation.

Does this sound like us?? We, the humans, at the top of the food chain? HUMANS are the only species who *intentionally* destroy each other! Humans kill humans because they don't like the color of their skin, don't agree with their beliefs, and want their possessions. Humans kill each other for no reason at all. Humans kill humans in the name of GOD!? What kind of GOD condones killing???

It is the unawakened human that will continue to plan and execute the most heinous monstrosity of mass murder under the guise of "to better the planet."

The only *sane* conclusion is humans are *insane*.

CHAPTER 28

Words Have Power

Of all sad words of tongue or pen, the saddest are these,
'It might have been.'
—*John Greenleaf Whittier*

"That doesn't sound that bad!" How many times have you heard someone say this after recapping what someone had said to you that you felt was critical and offensive? After hearing that remark, you probably said in your defense, "It was their tone! They used a tone!!" After all, you were there. You were the one having the conversation—not only did you feel the sting of the biting words, but you felt the *emotion* behind the words. You also felt the *intention* of the words directed to you. Yes, we can tell if someone is giving us a backhanded compliment. We can sense if a person is saying something to us sarcastically. We know if an apology is genuine or not. We all have the ability to feel the power of the energy behind words that are spoken and even read.

Words are very powerful. They carry a certain frequency, vibration, and emotion. When we say things, our words resonate emotions and intentions. If we intend for our words to have a negative impact, the person will feel this. If we want our words to sting, they will. I can tell when someone makes a comment to me if they mean it in a derogatory way.

When people speak to us with love and respect, we can feel this being projected behind their choice of words. We sense their heart-felt intention of love and respect when they speak to us. Conversely, if the person harbors anger and rage for us, it does not matter what they say because we can still feel the "hidden" anger, even if the words spoken may contradict this message.

For instance, I live in Atlanta, and there is a comical stereotype of Southern women being able to make a nasty comment with a smile plastered on their face, as if saying, "It can't be meant nasty . . . I'm smiling!" We can see the wicked Southern wench (kidding) smiling, but this cannot mask the vibration of the words, nor the tone and the intention behind the words. We have all been in a situation where someone may have made a comment to us, and we have felt the meaning behind the words even if they were hidden with a smile or cutesy wink. We do know if the comment was meant to be hurtful or said out of love. Sometimes we just don't want to trust what we know because we can't believe someone could intentionally be so mean.

Words in a Book Carry Energy Too

When you read this book, behind the words are my thoughts and intentions that I wanted the reader to receive. Thoughts and intentions are energy that the reader absorbs, not just the words. As I write each word, it is infused with the energy of my thoughts, intention, and emotion. *The words are being written with my intention of healing and awakening the reader. This is energy transference.* Written and spoken words—even unspoken thoughts—transmit energy, too. There is an energy transfer in all that we do. This is why when I would hold the signed copy of Eric's book *The Reconnection* in my hands, I would feel a pulsing that was more pronounced than when I would hold the unsigned copy.

Words Can Spread like a Weed

Gossip is powerful. Gossip is hurtful and a low vibration energy. Gossip changes our perception of how we view someone, often times in an instant. I'm going to use this hypothetical story as an example to get my point across:

Let's say Susan has a boss that she adores and respects. We'll call him Jack. Jack has always treated Susan fairly and has never been anything but respectful, kind, and appreciative of her hard work. The dream boss, so to speak. (This really is a fictitious story... haha.) The company has its yearly sales meeting at a beautiful resort in Orlando, Florida for the week. Susan is just getting out of the shower to get ready to meet everyone for breakfast before the first day of meetings and is suddenly startled by Pat Benatar's "Hit Me With Your Best Shot" ringtone blaring from her cell phone. The early morning call is from Cindy, another sales rep, who also works for Jack.

"Susan! You won't believe what I just witnessed! Diane was leaving Jack's room!! I was walking down the hallway at 5 a.m. to the elevator to go on my morning jog. She didn't see me, though,

She sneaked into her room two doors down!" Cindy does not give Susan a chance to say anything ... still hootin' and hollerin', carrying on about how this must be how Diane was recently promoted to a sales manager.

Jack married his college sweetheart, and Susan had heard his wife, Emma, is eight months pregnant with twins. Suddenly, Susan changes her view of her boss. She now thinks he is a total scumbag cheating on his pregnant wife, with twin boys on the way! All Susan feels now is disgust because Diane was recently promoted at work. Now she sees her as a trashy-no-talent-girl who obviously slept her way to the top.

With this new information, Susan quickly creates an action plan in her mind: snub slutty Diane and hate Jack. The next day back at the office, after the week-long sales meeting in sunny Orlando, Susan can barely look at Jack when he speaks to her. She has become unmotivated to do the quality of work for him that she did before because, as she states, when telling the story to another co-worker Danielle, "I've lost all respect for him!" The usual playful banter during the day with Diane is ignored. Susan now packs her lunch to avoid eating with her.

After a few weeks of Susan's highly noticeable lack of enthusiasm, less than stellar work, and late arrivals, Jack calls her into his office for a "heart to heart" to ask what is wrong. Susan does not want Jack to know "the truth" of what she knew. She feels like this is a sensitive subject and does not want to get involved in Jack's personal "affairs" so to speak. Susan quickly suspects her job is in jeopardy, and since she was no longer happy there, she turns in her resignation.

A few months later, at a local bar, Susan runs into Cindy, the girl who originally shared the "hookup" story of Jack and Diane with her at the sales meeting in Orlando. Cindy has already had a few drinks and confides in Susan that she started that rumor about Jack. "I wanted to screw him over because I interviewed for the same promotion and Diane got the job!

"Scrreeewww Jack!!" she drunkenly slobbers into her vodka tonic. Cindy, in her inebriated stupor, laughs and says, "Do you think I would wake up at 5 a.m. for a morning jog? I hate exercise!!!"

Through the Eyes of the Gossiper

This is the power of gossip. Susan sees Jack and Diane through Cindy's eyes of lies and deceit, and feels so betrayed and disgusted that she shares these lies to almost everyone who works for Jack. Susan tells Danielle, her best friend at work, that Jack is cheating on his "preggie wife" with Diane. Now Danielle sees Jack and Diane through Susan's eyes, and her perception of both Jack and Diane instantly shifts. When Danielle sees Katie in the break room grabbing a cup of coffee, she walks over to chat. You know how it goes from here. The story gets more distorted as each storyteller changes and enhances the narrative with their emotions, their intentions, and personal distorted views. Each time the story is repeated, the receiver feels the intention of the new storyteller and how his/her personal judgments come through the story.

Just think how many times we heard a comment about someone and instantly viewed them differently? It doesn't matter how long we knew that person, or even how we felt about them before.

We now see the person through the eyes of another—the gossiper. This is the intent of the gossiper. Gossip is hurtful. Gossip is a weed spreading out of control.

"Doggie Art"

Here's another example: Let's say a new neighbor just moves in across the street from me. I have not met the family yet, but I want to go over there to introduce myself. "Have you met the new neighbors? I thought I'd say hello. . . ." I tell another neighbor, Emily. Perhaps she replies, "Oh, I see that lady walk her Great Dane every day, and she never picks up the poop in the yard. Just leaves it there and walks on." Who knows whether this is accurate? I don't know if this is true or not, but right away I am thinking, *I don't want to be friends with someone who is inconsiderate,* and I decide I'm not going over there to meet the new family. So . . . here we are in this situation again. I don't know if this story is true. Yet now, I see this neighbor through Emily's eyes. Just think if I start telling this story to other neighbors with my own little added comments and embellishments to keep it fresh and interesting, "Can you believe that neighbor keeps letting her big dog make these gigantic *poop piles* in my yard, and leaves it there to make *doggie art*?!"

SEEK Your Own TRUTH

Wouldn't things be different if people sought out their own truth? Why are we so quick to believe what other people say about someone without seeing it with our own eyes or even having a conversation about it? Just think if Susan did speak up when Jack asked her what was wrong. She did not necessarily have to give up the source of the gossip, but at least Jack could have explained his side and Susan could have decided the validity of the situation.

Gossip Is Not Bathed in Love

Many of us have had situations at work where a coworker, whether it was jealousy or another reason, may have passed along gossip. We experience gossip among even our closet friendships. We all know gossip can destroy a person's credibility and reputation. Gossip is not bathed in love. This is not the foundation of love and respect. Gossip is intended to tarnish. The person spreading the gossip does not care if it is true or not. *The seed is planted in the mind of the listener.* The seed grows and roots are spread in the mind, until it is firmly planted. The water and fertilizer used to accelerate the growth is the continuation of the story—from one person to another. Each time the story is told it becomes more distorted as the new storyteller's beliefs, judgments, and emotions come through in the words. Gossip is a fast growing weed!

Gossip is a weed that keeps growing and spreading out of control until it is pulled out of the ground and destroyed.

Truth Is the Weed Killer

Gossip keeps spreading until it is pulled out and destroyed with the TRUTH. The truth is the weed killer that stops the gossip from spreading any further. There are people who love to gossip. To them, it is a form of harmless entertainment. Maybe in a way it validates their self-esteem by being viewed as the person who is always "in the know." The way to stop them from gossiping is to STOP them. If you act like you don't care and don't get excited and don't ask questions, you take the fun out of it. You are no longer the "fun person" to "share" their stories with. If you find it to direct and hurtful to say, "I don't like to gossip," or "I prefer to seek my own truth," or "I don't believe in spreading gossip." Just walk away. Do . . . something. Here is something you can do—if you hear something, and it distorts your view of the person— *ask* the person what the gossip was about.

Start a Conversation

Believe me; people would rather you ask them if something is true or to say you heard something about them than just treating them differently or avoiding them altogether without them knowing why. I know I would like to have that courtesy. How would you feel? Wouldn't you want to have a candid conversation about gossip that is spread about you as opposed to people reacting differently toward you and having no idea why? Shouldn't your side of the story be heard?

Why do people feel the need to spread gossip? People spread gossip because they in some way want to hurt the object of the gossip, defame the character, or denigrate a person's reputation. The gossiper may convince him/herself it is only harmless entertainment. Oftentimes, the person may feel the information "won't go anywhere," so it's okay. But this is rarely the case! One person confided in another person who then confides in another and so on and so on. . . .

This, of course, does not mean if you heard someone doing harm, stealing, breaking the law, molesting a child, etc. that you ignore this information and don't tell anyone. Common sense and good judgment of what follow-up course of action to take always prevails.

I will leave you with this wonderful quote.

"Great minds discuss ideas. Average minds discuss events. Small minds discuss people."
—*Eleanor Roosevelt*

People who are focused on accomplishing great things in the world do not spend the time and energy to destroy someone's reputation for fun or revenge.

This is why I love Eleanor Roosevelt's quote. She said this beautifully!

CHAPTER 29

Why Do We Forgive?

You have been criticizing yourself for years and it hasn't worked.
Try approving of yourself and see what happens.
—Louise L. Hay

Why is it important to forgive? It seems as though we hear this mantra over and over. "Forgive! Forgive!" as though this will solve all of our problems, and then suddenly, without warning, at the moment of our "forgiveness" we will feel free and light as all our burdens float away into the stratosphere, out of sight and out of mind.

We forgive for many reasons, which revolve around helping ourselves by releasing our pain and suffering so we can heal. To forgive is to help us live our life to *our* fullest potential. If we keep dwelling on events over and over that caused us emotional/physical pain, these memories will manifest as physical illness and a spiritual imbalance. Forgiveness is not about someone harming you, and now you are being expected to love this person and say, "Everything is okay." This is not forgiveness.

Release the Attachment

Forgiveness is letting go of the *attachment* to the situation or the person that harmed you—whether this harm is physical, emotional, mental, or spiritual. **I release the pain of the event, and I am ready to release the attachment to the person or situation and heal.** This is what it means to let go and move on. This is what forgiveness means. When you forgive someone for an injustice or a wrongdoing, you are not condoning it. You are not saying what you did and what happened was okay. When you are consumed with strong emotions of hatred and revenge, you are *energetically attached* to that person or situation. You are thinking about this constantly. Every time you ruminate and continually replay the events in your mind, *you are giving it more energy.* You become consumed by this experience; it is all you think about and becomes all you know. Then it encompasses your life preventing you from moving forward. You will be spiritually stagnant until you release this energy.

Think about how much time you spend every day brooding about a particular situation. When you do this, your cells are not getting messages for life—they are getting messages for dis-ease. Your life becomes dominated by these thoughts and emotions as you re-live the experience. Your cells react to these constant messages of anger, hatred, hostility, revenge, or negative emotion that you are hanging onto. Your immune system is listening and responding as well.

The message is: I am angry; I want revenge; I am full of hate. You are becoming ill—maybe even seriously ill. Every time you think about a past hurt, you are re-energizing these thoughts. You are investing your energy into a past hurt rather than focusing on the present. Instead of being in the NOW, you are stuck in the past and creating destruction to yourself emotionally, physically, and spiritually. You will end up physically sick, emotionally in pain, spiritually halted. This is what you are releasing: the attachment to these low vibrational energies of the past hurt.

Forgiveness is releasing the attachment you have to this person or situation.

There is a continuous and constant attachment to the person or situation until you let go of the emotional drain of "mental repeat." Your full power to create the life you want is in the present moment, to live in the NOW. By doing this, your focus and energy is on what is happening each moment in your present life, not continually sending your energy backward. This is not where your power is. Your power is in your present life.

Think of being attached by a string to the person who harmed you. *Forgiveness is breaking the string that is attaching you.* This is forgiveness: breaking the string and walking away with *your energy.* You are not saying you love this person. You are not saying what you did to me was okay. You are not saying the people involved should go unpunished. You are giving the situation up to God to make amends and saving yourself from an illness and possibly an autoimmune disorder, heart disease, cancer, and other chronic illnesses. You are finally allowing yourself to heal on a physical and cellular level as well as spiritually and emotionally. Spiritually, you will be ready to receive more light, raise your vibration, and attract more wonderful things into your life. On a mental level, you are healing emotionally while allowing more energy and light to infuse your physical being so that you can be a vessel for love—which is your true essence.

When you are stuck in this vicious cycle of obsessing with these negative thoughts, you lower your vibration and attract things in your life of a lower vibration. Your energy is being expended on these past attachments. So instead of having the full energy to enjoy your life as it is now, you are drained and exhausted and do not know why. Your greatest light and vibration and ENERGY are highest when you are in the NOW. Stay focused in the present.

This is very difficult—to finally let go. You will be sick and tired of it all, depressed with your life, and wanting to live again. One day, you will decide that *now* is the day to do this.

To FORGIVE Is to SAVE YOURSELF

Forgiveness is saving yourself. This is your motivation. This is the gift you are giving your soul. When we don't forgive, we remain the victim. We give the perpetrator power over us every day with continued thoughts of hated, revenge, anger, and injustice. Energetically, we are drained. We will continue to play the victim of hopelessness and despair. Is it worth it? You will spend the rest of your life stuck in time, never moving forward, constantly replaying this role.

Sometimes we just have to give it up to God and know that justice *will* be served. In the karmic law of the Universe, there is a reaction to every action. This is universal law of balance. Keep in mind that one lifetime is just a snippet of existence. We have many lifetimes as opportunities to learn and grow. If you see someone who harmed you, and it seems as though they have the best life—don't judge this. We may experience an unpleasant situation as part of our growth or karmic lesson as well. All karmic debts will be paid, even if it is in a subsequent lifetime. There will be atonement for any wrongdoing. This is the balance of the Universe. Another phrase describing karma: We reap what we sow. *What we create will return back to us.* This is the Law of the Circle, which is karma.

If you decide you are not ready to address the emotional issues, the symptoms will eventually manifest as illness in the physical body. Your body responds to the messages it receives and *reacts.* An example of this is how negative thoughts such as jealously, hate, anger, and fears affect the thymus gland, which is located in the chest area behind the breastbone (sternum). The thymus gland processes white blood cells and converts these cells into T-cells—the T is for thymus. These white blood cells or T cells are our first line of defense toward fighting off an infection. When we have ongoing negative thoughts and emotions, our thymus gland weakens and doesn't work optimally. This constant stress and emotional turmoil decreases the function of our immune system, which is why we are more prone to illness, infections, and disease.

Remember when you were a kid, and your mom yelled, "Put shoes on when you go outside! You'll catch a cold!" or "Don't go outside without a coat, you'll get sick!" Better advice from Mom would have been, "Keep up your immunity so that you won't get sick." We are all exposed to viruses and bacteria, but it is when our immune system is lowered that we get sick. When I am run down or stressed from work, my throat starts to hurt and then I usually get a cold or some type of upper respiratory infection. Why is it that one person in a household gets a cold, and the rest of your family doesn't catch it? Their immune system is heightened. This is why some people may get the flu from a person at work while another in close contact may be unaffected. If you are run down and stressed, you will be more susceptible to "catching the germs" that are going around. Yes . . . even if you do have your coat on.

Our Cells Can Hold ANGER

Have you ever been so angry you could feel your entire body tense? If you looked at yourself in a mirror, would you see both your fists clenched into a tight ball, face getting apple red, furrowed brows that look like a "before" photo for Botox? It's probably not a pretty sight on the outside or the inside—this physical manifestation of your anger occurs internally as well. Anger blocks our energy flow. The longer you maintain this emotion, the longer your body suffers and creates an energy blockage.

- When our cells hold onto anger; *we are anger.*
- We are cells are bathed in love; *we are love.*
- When are cells are sick; *we are sick.*

Our thought is the conductor directing the orchestra. *Do you want a beautiful symphony playing? Or, would you prefer constant, loud, and disjointed non-rhythmic banging?*

In section I, chapter 7, I discussed how anger and frustration cause the DNA to wind tighter. Anger caused the DNA to become "wound up" just as we get "wound up" when we are irate. When you've been uptight, you've heard someone say, "Don't get so wound up! Don't get so wound up over the kids screaming! Don't get so wound up over being late for dinner with friends!"

Our cells are continually getting messages from our thoughts and from our emotions. Our cells are always listening to our spoken dialogue and our inner thoughts. When we silently talk to ourselves, our DNA is still listening. This is why it is so important to give yourself messages of self-love, whether you do it silently or aloud.

Just think what would happen to our cells if we were constantly stressed and angry. We would spend the majority of our lives with our DNA strands being wound tight and becoming shorter. Can you see how stress and anger can be the cause of illness and dis-ease? "Dis-ease" is the opposite of "ease." This is why you may see the word *dis-ease* hyphenated to show the difference of the body's natural state *ease* of balance and harmony. Dis-ease is when our DNA is getting messages of anger, hate, frustration, and stress and is *tightened*. Ease is when our DNA is getting messages of love, peace, and harmony and is *relaxed*.

Our emotions don't lie. We can verbalize one thing and feel another. For instance, how many times have you answered "Good" or "Great!" when someone asked how you were doing? We may not be emotionally or physically well that day, but we are conditioned to know that most people really don't care and don't want a long diatribe of how we really feel. It's as though we're expected to say, "Fine."

When We Forgive We Relax Our DNA

When we forgive others and forgive ourselves, we give our immune system a boost. If we hold on to repressed anger, we are susceptible to illness because we impair our immune function. This is why one family member may get a cold or flu virus and become sick while the rest of the exposed family is fine. *It is our susceptibility to become sick that we become sick.*

When we release these harbored negative emotions, we release the blockage of our immune system. I like to think of this as an *immune system catharsis*. We are free, and our immunity is again kick-started and bolstered.

How Do You Know When You Have Truly Forgiven?

Have you ever experienced a migraine headache and felt so utterly miserable—then it went away, and you seemed to feel better than ever?! This feeling of ultimate release is when you know you have truly forgiven. You feel free. Your focus and energy has shifted to YOU! You have more energy. Do you realize how much of your energy is drained when you focus on your injustice and hatred, and possibly self-loathing for that matter, especially if you are playing the victim and blaming yourself for what happened? How do you expect your immune system to heal your body when the majority of your energy is being directed to a past attachment?

When you truly forgive, you feel unstuck. Your mind is no longer replaying the event over and over. You are focused on the present moments of your life and moving forward, not backward. You are motivated to live your life again and excited to do things that bring you joy. Your heart feels lighter: *a freedom of burden.* Oh, and by the way, your DNA starts to finally *unwind* and *relax.* This is how you "save yourself" when you forgive.

CHAPTER 30

We Eat ENERGY

If this is coffee, please bring me some tea; but if this is tea,
please bring me some coffee.
—Abraham Lincoln

Since we are energy beings, we need an energy source to sustain ourselves. This energy comes from the sun, the Universal Energy, and from our food and water. When we eat food that vibrates and has a frequency, we consume energy.

Whole foods such as fruits and vegetables provide greater energy and a higher nutritional value than processed foods with refined sugars. These types of foods are considered "junk foods" because that is essentially what they are when you look at the life force they have. The vibration is low. Instead of adding fuel in the form of high vibrational energy and nutrition to the body, junk food depletes us.

Our bodies actually work harder to metabolize and digest this low vibrational and nutritional food.

Excess sugar is poison to the body and causes inflammation in all of our cells. The body does not even know what to do with it. Back in the day when we were hunters, we lived on unprocessed foods. We ate lean meats and survived on plant life, plenty of fresh fruits, and vegetables. This is still how our cells function at their best. Our bodies are most efficient when we eat healthy whole foods. Not only are we able to metabolize them better, we have a greater supply of energy. This is why we often feel sluggish and drained after consuming a lot of junk and fast-food. We need energy to function just like a car needs gas to drive. If you put the wrong gas in your car, it will be sluggish. We will also function poorly with the wrong food source as energy.

Our food source is so much different than when I was a kid. When I was growing up, the apple didn't fall to far from the tree. This means that once the fruits and vegetables were gathered, they arrived in the local stores quicker and had a higher nutritional content and energy supply. It was very common back then to see local farmers with stands of their produce on the side of the road. Every summer, I would look forward to these fresh fruit and vegetable stands from the local farmers. This was the good ole days when produce was fresh off the farm. Now, very little of it is fresh. Most produce is sprayed with pesticides and harsh chemicals and shipped from warehouses over many days before it reaches supermarkets.

Most of the time when I eat fruit, it hardly tastes like fruit unless it's organic. It seems to have a weird chemical after-taste no matter how much I rinse it. I try to buy organic produce whenever possible; the food is a little more expensive, but worth it. The fruit tastes natural and not like chemicals. It's amazing how many kids have never had fresh fruit and vegetables. My daughter had a friend over from school, and I asked her if she would like some blueberries. "What's a blueberry?" she responded. I laughed. I thought she was playing with me. Nope . . . the kid never had a blueberry. I rattled off a number of different fruits. Nope . . . didn't have those before either. If kids were not introduced to fruits and vegetables at home, how would they know?

Animals Are ENERGY That We Eat

The animals that we eat carry energy and a frequency as well. If the animal has been abused and neglected, it would have a lower energy and vibration. If the animal is slaughtered in an inhumane way, we are ingesting the fear and trauma in the form of energy from the flesh of the animal that we are eating. We are ingesting the animal's energy and vibration. This may seem fascinating, but when we eat a plant or animal source, *we absorb transference of energy.* This is why it is so important to treat our animals that are going to be slaughtered humanely, not to mention all the ethical reasons involved with treating animals with compassion and kindness. Animals do have emotions, awareness, and consciousness.

Plants, animals, and humans have a life force. If we eat diseased plants that have been sprayed with toxic chemicals and pesticides, then we ingest poisons. When we eat meat from an animal that was cared for inhumanely, we are introducing this vibration into our body as we eat the meat. Think of it in this way—if you have chickens crammed into a tiny, filthy pen, laying in their own feces, never allowed daylight, are not free to roam and get some exercise, are sick and injected with massive doses of antibiotics, what do you think the energy will be like in our body when we eat this chicken?!

We are eating the energy of this sick chicken. We are eating the energy of an animal that when slaughtered is experiencing fear, trauma, and suffering. These emotions alter the energy of the animal just as these same emotions alter the energy in humans. Sick chickens lay sick eggs. When we eat eggs of chickens that are not cared for, we eat eggs that have a low vibrational energy. This is why I buy cage-free organic eggs without antibiotics. I want to enjoy an omelet with a high vibrational energy. I know that the energy of how the chicken was cared for, and how the chicken was slaughtered, *will* affect the energy of the food I am eating.

If we eat disease, we become diseased.

There Is an ENERGY Transfer in the Food We Eat

Fresh, wholesome food has the highest life force, but by the time the food is shipped to your grocery store, it loses about a third of its nutrients. When the food is processed and canned, it loses additional energy. By the time you cook the food, you are lucky if you have about a quarter of the life force that was originally in the food. This is why people adopt a raw food program because raw foods contain a higher life force and have a much higher nutritional content. You are eating living food.

When we eat food, our vibration either becomes higher or lower. If you eat chemical laden food, your vibration will be lowered. If you eat at the fast-food chains, the quality and vibration of your food is low. I recently read that McDonalds french fries have 19 different ingredients. Yuck!! You think this is food? You can make this in a laboratory! *Real food has a small number of ingredients.* If I make french fries at home, I can make it with just three ingredients: potatoes, salt, and oil. If you can't pronounce all of the ingredients listed for the food you eat and have no idea what they are, why would you put that in your mouth?! Next time you buy that frozen pizza at the grocery store, read the ingredients. You will be amazed, to say the least. There could be anywhere from 30-40 ingredients listed of "who knows what."

Food stored in cans have very little nutritional value. Essentially, we are now eating food with very little life force left. The food is not "alive." Check it out for yourself. Go to your pantry and look at the expiration date on your canned food. My mom used to heat up canned green beans at almost every meal for us at dinner. I loved it! I thought they were delicious. There was something appealing to me about the softness and sogginess of these beans as opposed to the crisp, fresh green beans. What can I say? As a kid, I certainly had a different awareness than I do now. A can of green beans lasts about two years. Real food is not made to last that long. If I buy fresh green beans, they may be good for about a week before they start to turn brown. Frozen fruits and vegetables are definitely a better choice than canned food, which usually contains a high level of sodium and often times will contain hidden MSG. As a fun project, next time you are in the grocery store, look at some of the expiration dates on the various canned food items. You will be amazed as you see two to three yearlong expiration dates. I refer to this as "bomb shelter food." This is what you want to stock up on and place in your underground shelter in case of a nuclear fallout, and not fill up your kitchen pantry.

LOVE Makes Food Taste Better

When my kids have a cold, I make them homemade chicken noodle soup. I tell them that this is a "healing soup" with the vibration to help them feel better. I *prepare the soup with love* and place my *intention* on healing and helping my kids feel better. Morgan and Brandon don't understand how, but they always feel a relief of their symptoms after they eat my soup. Intuitively, people have been aware of how much better they feel after a good home-cooked meal. Even a home-cooked meal from a restaurant does not compare to the energy of food cooked with gratitude and appreciation from the people who love you.

We know that LOVE is the highest vibration of the Universe, so when you mindfully cook food with love, you raise the vibration of the food you eat. When you cook with fresh whole foods and organic food you are working with a higher vibration of food energy as well. When you give gratitude for the food you eat, since gratitude is a form of love, you raise the vibration of the food. This is the reason for "saying grace" before a meal. You are expressing gratitude for the food you have that sustains you. Gratitude does not have to be in the form of a long prayer said aloud. You can express this gratitude silently with a simple thought, "I am grateful for this food." Remember, thoughts are energy too, and the Universe receives this expression of "thank you."

Eating with Awareness

Do you multi-task while you eat: sitting at your computer working, reading a book, chatting on the phone, checking updates on Facebook? Think about how many times a day we mindlessly eat. We eat in front of the TV. We eat while we are driving around in our cars with the radio blasting. We are so busy multitasking that we do not take the time to become aware of the pleasure in eating because we don't even pay attention to it.

We are not consciously involved in the *experience of eating*. We are not enjoying the taste, the texture, or all of the delicate, intricate flavors. We have lost the mindfulness that we need to feel satiated from our food. We are not *present* when we eat. Our mind is completely focused elsewhere. How many times have you eaten something and thought, *Did I eat that bag of chips? I can't remember.* Or have you ever said, "Did I eat lunch today?" We shovel food in our mouths, and suddenly the entire bag of chips is gone.

When we eat with lack of awareness, we over-eat. *When we eat with awareness, we feel the emotional connection with our food.* Eating should be a fun and emotional experience. We keep craving more food and more variety of food because we did not give the time and attention to sit down, relax, and eat with full attention. If you eat slowly, savor every delicious bite. You will feel satisfied even when you eat much smaller portions.

Eat like the French

The French people have leisurely meals compared to the speed eating of Americans. Often times we eat with our food on our lap as we are driving or watching TV. We aren't paying attention to how much we eat. We are not paying attention to whether we feel full. We just eat the entire portion that is in front of us. Why? Because it's there. If we eat food in a bag, we have to eat until the bag is empty.

The French eat what they want, but they eat smaller portions and feel satisfied. They don't feel deprived. They eat with mindfulness by sitting down to a leisurely meal and savoring and enjoying each bite. Americans, for the most part, usually speed-eat large portions. The French eat dessert, too! Just a very small portion satisfies their sweet craving, not a huge piece of pie or an entire banana split.

If you have ever eaten at an authentic French restaurant, your meal had several courses—usually, an appetizer, salad, entree, and dessert, but the portion sizes were very small. The food is usually delicious, flavorful, and rich. You feel satisfied instead of stuffed. It's about portion control. Some people may leave and feel gypped like they didn't get value for their money and left hungry. The French eat real food—real butter, real cheese, and good chocolate. They don't eat as much processed and fast-foods as Americans do.

I realize I am making quite a few generalizations here regarding how we Americans eat versus how the French eat, but the point I am making is that for the most part in this country we don't savor the food experience and take the time to enjoy this food energy that sustains us. Consequently, we don't truly feel satisfied after a meal, and we want to eat more. The French people don't feel deprived. They eat what they want; they just don't eat a lot of what they want. The food is rich, tasty, and satisfying, so they eat less of it.

It's not the quantity of food you eat but the quality of your food experience that will satisfy you.

Make a Rat Fat with MSG

Did you know that if researchers want to study how an obesity drug works in rats and mice, they inject them with MSG (monosodium glutamate) so they can make them fat? The fact that MSG makes mice obese is well known in the scientific community and the food industry as well. There are over a hundred studies of rodents being injected with MSG to create fat rats. How does MSG make mice fat? The MSG causes the pancreas to release more insulin. When this happens, the increased insulin levels signal the body to store fat.

What is MSG? It is used as a "flavor enhancer," which causes us to feel hungrier and eat more. Almost every food in boxes, cans, and packages (even frozen) at your grocery store contains MSG. The food industry loves MSG. We eat more. We buy more food! Also, since MSG *over-stimulates* our taste buds, bad food tastes better.

MSG is in almost every processed food. The majority of fast-food that we eat is loaded with it. Even most of the popular restaurant chains serve already prepared food loaded with MSG. I am mentioning this in my book because we really are what we eat. We nourish our bodies with food. This is our life force, the energy that nourishes our bodies and keeps us alive. Isn't it a good thing to know what type of energy we are putting in our bodies? We need healthy food, clean water, and sunshine if we want to be balanced and healthy. *It we eat food that is designed to keep us fat and sick, we will be fat and sick.*

It's about being aware of what we eat to maintain good health. If we try to eat a healthy meal from a local restaurant chain or fast-food loaded with MSG, we are sabotaging our own efforts of "eating healthy" as we are likely consuming huge amounts of sodium and MSG. Even many of the so-called "healthy salads" are loaded with MSG. If you think your are eating healthy because you walk down the frozen food aisle of your grocery store and avoid the high calorie frozen lasagnas, assorted pies, cakes, and pizza, and opt for the frozen "lean" and "healthy" choices, you are eating MSG. This "lean" frozen dinner with MSG also has anywhere from 500-1000 mg of sodium. This is not helping you to keep weight off. The recommended daily total allowance for sodium is less than 2400 mg per day. With one frozen dinner, you have almost reached the maximum healthy limit. Excess sodium not only causes that excess water weight as you retain more water, this can also cause high blood pressure as well.

The best places to eat are the restaurants that freshly prepare the foods from scratch. If you want to avoid MSG, then avoid KFC (Kentucky Fried Chicken). They are by far one of the worst offenders of MSG overload in their menu items! When I was in my 20s, I used to eat occasionally at KFC. Usually, someone would bring a bucket of chicken to a picnic or to the lake if we were boating. I could never figure out why I would devour every crumb of that chicken. I couldn't get enough of it! No matter how many pieces of chicken I ate, I was still hungry. Now I know why. All that MSG made me ravenous. My fingers were in my mouth devouring every scrap as I was contemplating licking the bucket! That's MSG!

I have seen grocery store items that list on the front of the package "no MSG." Then I will read the ingredient label, and the item will have *MSG, but it will be hidden under a different name* such as yeast extract, hydrolyzed vegetable protein, autolyzed yeast, or sodium caseinate. Do not be fooled. This is just a name game. The item still contains MSG. The food industry will label on the front of the package "no MSG" and the ingredients may still contain MSG in another form. The food industry knows we have started to "catch on" to the misleading—no MSG labels—so now they may simply hide the MSG ingredient under "natural flavors." If you do a search on the Internet for other names for MSG, a long list will come up. Check the back label list of the ingredients of items you purchase before you just throw things in your cart.

MSG Makes Flavor INTENSE

Can you tell when you eat these foods if they have MSG? Have you ever eaten a packaged snack food and the flavor seems to "pop" in your mouth? The intense flavor seems to over-stimulate your taste buds. It's like the wow factor. This is usually MSG. I do not let my kids eat Doritos because of the MSG. They love the taste. Doritos comes in so many exotic, bold flavors and are very tasty. The "wow" when you take a crunchy bite is MSG. When you eat an item with MSG, it's hard to stop eating it until you have finished the entire bag.

If you have eaten fast-food or a snack food loaded with MSG and felt dizzy or had a headache, you may have been experiencing MSG toxicity. It can also cause numbness and tingling in hands and feet, sweating, heart palpitations, etc. Fun right? Even if you go to a Chinese restaurant, and they do not use MSG in their cooking. Guess what? The soy sauce naturally contains MSG. You may want to use another dipping sauce for your sushi as well. Soy sauce contains ~ 1000mg of sodium for just one tablespoon. If you have only two tablespoons of soy sauce, you have close to your recommended daily allowance of sodium.

Eating a "healthy" boxed frozen food meal may be counter-productive if it contains a high amount of MSG and sodium. If you are wondering why you have been eating healthy but still eating packaged and processed foods that seem to be good for you and are not losing weight even if you are exercising, read the food labels and check for hidden MSG. This could be part of the problem and not the solution for your healthy food choice that you had hoped for.

We Are What We Eat

We have all heard this before. We are what we eat so eat healthy . . . blah . . . blah . . . blah. If this is true, then why do most doctors still tell us that our health problems are not related to what we eat? When was the last time you went to your doctor with a health ailment and were asked what you eat? I never have. Ever!

Most dermatologists still tell their patients that foods do not cause acne. This myth was negated years ago. Even if these foods may not cause acne in some people, they will aggravate acne in those who are prone to acne by increasing oil production. There is so much anecdotal information and research linking dairy consumption to acne. Milk is loaded with hormones. As a result, these hormones cause the skin to produce more sebum, the skin becomes clogged, and bacteria forms, and you wake up with a pimple that you swear was not there yesterday!

Foods with a high glycemic index have shown to aggravate acne as well. This information has been researched and published.

The glycemic index for foods uses a scale of 0-100. The faster the sugar enters your bloodstream, the higher the glycemic index is for a certain food. For instance, these are some high glycemic index foods: cakes, pies, candy, donuts, pancakes, fruit juices, french fries, and bread. Foods with a high sugar content and processed carbohydrates such as snack chips, pretzels, crackers, and breakfast cereals are a few of the high sugar load foods. High glycemic foods make your insulin levels spike, which like dairy, cause more oil production. If you notice that your face is suddenly more oily than usual and looks like an oil slick your car left behind, then look at your diet as a potential culprit. There are also published studies linking gluten to acne, rashes, eczema, and other skin conditions. It makes no sense for dermatologists or any other physicians or laypersons to say that the foods we eat don't affect skin conditions. Of course, they can. Our skin is the largest organ of our body. We eliminate toxins through our skin.

Our skin shows signs of inflammation by reacting to what we put in our body. If the foods that we eat are not toxic to us, then why do we test for food allergies? It's because people have symptoms that can be traced to the food. Foods can even trigger an autoimmune disease in people who are sensitive. We have all heard of someone with a peanut allergy. Maybe we know someone with Celiac disease. You may be a person or know someone who is allergic to dairy, shellfish, or eggs. Some of these reactions are life-threatening. Many of us have more subtle symptoms that are not life-threatening but exist such as painful joints, brain fog, and headaches. We could also have damage internally to our organs as we also develop external symptoms. Skin conditions are just more of an obvious manifestation to food sensitivities because this large organ is visible.

There was a review paper published in the New England Journal of Medicine (NEJM) that linked fifty-five diseases to gluten.[43] In the past, we were led to believe that eating gluten could harm only people with Celiac disease. New information has shown that gluten can cause other illnesses that are not solely associated with the gut, which include psychiatric disorders such as anxiety, depression, schizophrenia, and neurological disorders such as migraines, autism, and dementia. Even dermatologic disorders have been linked to gluten (and dairy) such as rash, acne, and eczema.

If the foods we eat do not affect our health, then why have so many people cured themselves of illnesses and diseases with juicing and eating raw foods? There are countless reports of people having a remission of an illness just by changing their *food lifestyle* and eating a healthier diet.

Our food source is the energy that sustains energy beings: We the HUMAN. If we consume low energy vibration food as a source of nutrients for our body to function properly, it will not perform very well. Now that you have a greater awareness of how the fuel you eat will affect how your body will run; do you want to fill up with a high or a low performance fuel?

It takes a conscious choice to make a healthier choice.

CHAPTER 31

The Amazing Animals

The greatness of a nation and its moral progress can be judged by the way its animals are treated.
—*Mahatma Gandhi*

Are you an animal lover? Have you always had pets growing up? Do you think about and miss your pet while you are at work, doing errands, and on vacation? Do you prefer the company of your animals to people? Do you often show cute pics of your pets before the kid's pictures? Yes!!! To all of the above! I consider myself to be one of *these* people.

I have always been happier surrounded by my animals and really did not need an excessive amount of human interaction. With that being said, I am not a hermit by any means. I am working in sales and have plenty of social time. But, I know that I love being surrounded by my pets. My daughter is very social and needs to be with her friends constantly. She is certainly much happier around people and seems to get really down when she has too much alone time. I, on the other hand, have always preferred pets to people. When I was a kid, I didn't ask for toys and games for birthdays and holidays; I wanted a bunny or a guinea pig or a dog. I begged and pleaded until I got a pet. My dad would finally say yes! Even when I was a small child I could feel the unconditional love and gratitude of my dear animal friend.

As a child, I didn't understand why I felt so much better around my animals. I just knew that I did. I felt very "in tune" with my furry friends. It was as if I could sense their emotions and thoughts. I understood what they wanted to communicate to me. I knew that the love I had for animals was different than that of most other kids I knew in the neighborhood. The love and innate connection that I had with animals was always very apparent and noted with all my parents' friends. Throughout my childhood, they had all assumed that I was going to be a veterinarian one day and surround myself with animals.

I knew that this is something that I would not do. I had such a strong connection with animals that when I would see an animal in distress, I would become very distressed. It was as if I could take on the emotion of the animal. I could not bear to see an animal in pain or suffering. There are many people who seem happiest around their pets. This is not abnormal. There is nothing wrong with this. *Oftentimes, we feel more love, appreciation, and gratitude from our animal friends than our people friends.*

Animals Help Us Heal

Animals can give us a purpose in life when we may feel lonely and depressed as if we no longer have a place in this world. If we have a dog, we have to get out of bed in the morning. We have a responsibility; we have a life depending on us for food and care. We have to feed the dog and go to the grocery store for food. We have to take the dog out for walks. We can't just hide and let the world go on without us. Having a pet can give us a reason to continue when we may feel isolated and alone. We may no longer be someone's wife or husband. Maybe our kids are grown and have a life of their own, and we no longer feel the unconditional love of our family anymore. Having a pet provides company and the comfort of not being alone and feeling loved again.

When I have a bad day, I look forward to cuddling with my dog on my lap. I feel better immediately. You can talk to your pets. Animals are great therapists. They are great listeners and don't interrupt or try to give you advice. They are just there, fully present, and spending time with you. Studies have shown that when you pet your animal, your blood pressure and stress hormones are lowered. The "feel good" hormones are released, and help you to relax and elevate your mood. Your animals benefit from your love and attention as well. The same "feel good" hormones are released in your pet when you give them love and attention.

The love we feel from our cherished pet can help us cope better with the stress of everyday life. If we have a bad day, we feel our spirits lifted as soon as we pet and cuddle with our beloved animal friend. Animals help us maintain balance in our life. If you would rather spend time watching television or sitting at your computer for hours on end checking social media and your dog is tugging at your pant leg and barking non-stop because she wants you to take her on a long walk or play, you are forced to take a break, go outside, and get some exercise.

Animals Raise Our Vibration

When we pet and take care of our animal companions, our thoughts are based on LOVE. This unconditional love that we are projecting with our thoughts and emotions is very powerful. We are changing our frequency. Our frequency and our vibration are higher. We feel the love from our animals. The animals feel our love as well. Have you ever wondered if your animal knows how much you love them? Do they know how grateful you are to have them in your life? Absolutely! Your animal friends can feel the love you have for them just as we can feel how much our animal friends loves us.

There is an unspoken energy transference that takes place. This is the POWER OF LOVE. When we love, pet, and cuddle with them, our emotional state changes and our vibration is elevated. We are calmer, happier, and more at peace, and our cells respond to this state. Our immune system is heightened and more functional, so we are less prone to illness. The love we give and receive from our pets can bolster our immune system.

Our pets know our emotions. They are able to read our frequency. Have you ever been really sad or feeling depressed and your dog or cat came over and sat in your lap as if to offer comfort? *Our animal friends are more in tune with our thoughts and emotions than most humans are.* Our dogs seem to be able to sense when we are coming home. If your dog is there to greet you at the front door no matter what time you get home, it is because they can sense our intentions. They can pick up on our thoughts and emotions telepathically. This is why when we are thinking of taking our dog on a walk . . . they know! Your dog may already be at the door before you even find the leash.

When I am getting ready to take my dog to the vet and I call her name, she won't come! I see her sitting on the bed shaking. She knows! Now when I have to take my dog to the vet, I have a talk with her and let her know what I am doing. This calms her down. I tell her when I am taking her to the vet, and she actually enjoys the car ride, sticks her head out the window with her tongue hanging out of her mouth to catch the breeze instead of being curled up in the back seat of the car.

When she is going to the doggie hotel (kennel), I explain to her that we are going on vacation and tell her how many nights she will be there. When I am out of town, I send her love and I know she can sense it. Everyone has this ability to communicate with the animals in their lives. When you love your animals, you have a connection with them. *It is through this connection that you are in tune with their emotions.* You know when your pet is happy. You know when your pet is sad or not feeling well. Everyone has the capacity to do this. You are already doing this and may not even be aware that the information you are getting is from your pet.

Your dog can also sense when there is strife in the family. When I yell at my kids, my dog runs to hide in the closet and cowers. When the kids are fighting, or the parents are yelling, look at the dog. Oftentimes, the dog is hiding in a room or under a piece of furniture. Your animals respond to the dynamics of the emotions in your household just as the humans do who live there.

Friend or Foe

Our animals can sense when we approach them if we intend to harm them or love them. Animals can also sense fear and panic. If you approach a dog with fear or intention to harm, the dog will growl at you. When I was single and dating, I had a little white toy poodle that I absolutely adored. "Gucci" was the best judge of character. If she growled and barked incessantly at my date, I knew he was going to be a jerk. My "Gucci Pucci" (as I called her) was always right. I also got an opportunity to see how my date interacted with my little dog. If the guy made an effort to play with Gucci, petted her, and gave her attention, he was usually thoughtful and nice. I had one guy walk into my apartment, look at my adorable little poodle and say, "How long does a dog like that live??" Yup!!! He was a callous, egotistical jerk who treated everyone he encountered as though they were subservient to him, mostly because he had a good paying job and drove a Porsche. I have always said, "To love me is to love my dog."

Animals Don't Judge Us

Is there any wonder why some people really do prefer their pets to humans? *Animals don't judge us!* Our pets don't care how much money we make. Our pets don't care what we look like. Our pets don't care if we are fat or thin, attractive, or homely. They only care if we *love* them! Sometimes, I'll catch Goldye staring at me and wonder what she is thinking. She's not thinking she hates my sweater or wondering why I'm having a bad hair day. She is waiting for me to pet her and talk to her and give her attention.

Animals give us a sense of purpose, love us unconditionally, help us to calm down when we are stressed, provide emotional support when we need it, bring us so much joy, and keep us from going through life alone.

Do you think it is a coincidence that "dog" is "God" spelled backward?

Dogs, as well as our other pets, provide us with a great deal of emotional support and unconditional love. Friends come and go, but your animal friend is your best friend. Just don't ask to borrow money from them. I asked my dog Goldye for ten dollars, and she looked at me like I was crazy! Then I asked my kids and got the same look. Guess they learned it from the dog!

I can't think of a better way to end this chapter than with the quote by the beautiful and talented movie star, Elizabeth Taylor:

"Some of my best leading men have been dogs and horses."

CHAPTER 32

My Home Is Your Home

Buy land, they're not making it anymore.
—*Mark Twain*

Seven billion people on EARTH all live together and share the same Home. This is one crowded house! We are all dependent on planet Earth to survive. Mother Earth provides us with food, water, shelter, the air we breathe, and a place where we can evolve and experience life. Until the Earth is balanced and healthy, we cannot be fully balanced and healthy because we have a connection to her. It is up to us to take care of our Earth home.

Don't we honor and cherish the people who we love and value in our lives? When we recite marriage vows we agree to **love, honor, and cherish.** This is the same commitment we should have for Mother Earth. When it comes to our home, we defile where we live.

We have lost the respect for our home. We have lost the *sense of stewardship* for our planet. If we truly love our planet, we will take care of her. We will cherish her and treat her with respect like we would treat someone whom we dearly love.

Taking care of our home is our inherent obligation within the jurisdiction of our birthright. *If you are going to be born on a planet, you take care of that planet!*

Have you ever lived in a messy house full of clutter? You will definitely feel the stress. The energy throughout the house does not flow freely with all the untidiness. This is why we do "spring cleaning." We are getting rid of the old to make room for the new. I know when my house is messy and cluttered I am certainly not as relaxed as when my house is clean and a little more organized. I feel stressed as soon as I walk in, and I don't want to hang out at home. I want to leave! I also feel like I can't think as well when being around all the disorder. If I try to write, I become easily distracted.

For those of you who have a messy desk that you work from, try cleaning all the rummage and organizing it a little better and see how you feel when you sit down to work. Are you more relaxed? Are you more creative? Do ideas seem to come to you more easily? You can actually feel a difference when the energy around your workspace flows smoothly or is blocked by the stress of a disorganized space.

Think of how you feel when your home is clean and peaceful. You look forward to spending time there. It becomes a safe haven for you. You feel relaxed and content when you are there. Unfortunately, our Earth home is cluttered, polluted, violent, and dirty. Do you really want to live in a home like that? Well . . . guess what? You *do* live in a home like that!?

No matter where we might be, we are not separate from the Earth. Even when we are on an airplane, we are part of the Earth. When you leave your house to go to work, errands, or vacation, you are in another environment that affects how you feel; however, you don't leave the Earth when you are doing these activities. The Earth is our home 24/7. It is extremely stressful to live with war, poverty, hunger, and chaos. We have the resources and the power to change the environment we live in. There is certainly enough of us here to pitch in and help just like family members in your home pitch in to clean up!

We are ignorant creatures to think that our irreverence for our home does not affect us in our lifetime. We are creating our own demise! We pollute our air with carbon. We breathe this air. We pollute our water with oil and chemicals. We drink this water. We pollute our food with toxins, chemicals, GMOs, and hormones. We eat this food. Can you see how cleaning up this planet should be of our highest priority?

We have become what we have created—TOXIC. Our Earth is sick. We are sick. When we poison our environment—we poison ourselves. If we destroy our home—we destroy ourselves. If we continue on this path of destruction of our home, we will have nowhere to live. We cannot continue to be in denial that cleaning up our planet and maintaining a pristine home is our highest priority. If we find a way to work together in *cooperation instead of competition,* we would come together and create a healthy planet. If we focus our time and attention on healing the planet as opposed to expending our energy and resources on war, we could have a beautiful vibrant, healthy planet, and a chance for PEACE on Earth.

CHAPTER 33

Life Is a Gift

Yesterday is history, tomorrow is a mystery, today is God's gift,
that's why we call it the present.

—*Joan Rivers*

There is a reason why you are holding this book in your hands and reading it. You are reading *Excuse Me! Your Energy is Showing* because you are *ready to receive* this book at this time in your life. Just as I was *ready to receive* Dr. Eric Pearl's book *The Reconnection* when an Angel was waiting for me at the bookstore and placed Eric's book in my hands.

What are you ready for? The same thing I was ready for back in June of 2003. You are ready to receive information that *will awaken a vibration within you that is already there*. What has changed over the years? Humans have evolved. The vibration on the planet is higher now because we have become more aware. We are starting to remember our divine origin. *My book is helping you to wake up and remember who you really are.* Just as Eric's book helped me to remember that I am a healer and should be doing this work again.

Life truly is a gift from God. We are given this gift to come to this planet to *experience* life so that we evolve. We have a "playground" where we can create and learn and remember the origin of who we really are. This gift is given to us as spiritual beings with unconditional love from God. This energy—this light—is love. The word **evol**ve is love.

The timing of events that happen in our lives is so important. If I wrote this book ten years ago, people probably would have not connected with it. People didn't *speak energy* then like they do now. If you pay attention to how we talk, you will see how often we use Energy in everyday speech: "I didn't like his energy," or "I don't want to put that energy out into the Universe." I turn on the television and hear comments about Energy, whether it is a reality show, talk show, sitcom, etc. It does not matter the format. **We are all speaking ENERGY.** This is a good thing. This means we are now aware of Energy in our life as something real and tangible.

We are starting to understand our true inherent power as creators, and because of this, we can shape the energy to work for us. Isn't it a wonderful feeling to know that we are in control of our lives as opposed to feeling as though life is controlling you?

We Are Meant to Be Unique

It is possible to express one's true nature through a multitude of avenues. I have chosen writing. When I write, I am able to express my true self. I feel as though I have a canvas to express how I see the world. I have a unique opportunity to show everyone my perception of the world I live in. This is my reality playing out according to my beliefs and my awareness—which is constantly changing.

I am expressing my uniqueness.

Why do we spend so much time trying to conform and be like everyone else? **We are all a unique and individualized soul expressing our divine nature as a spark of light from our Creator.** We are not meant to be a carbon copy of each other.

We are here to express our divinity. We are here to let our unique, beautiful soul shine with our unique divine light.

We Play Follow the Leader

I always think it's interesting how I see two lines for the parking garage exit to pay; the one line will have five to six cars, the other zero. Why? Because people just follow each other. We don't even think for ourselves anymore. As soon as I pull into the lane with no cars, I see others follow. How many times have you seen this? It could be a movie ticket line or anything for that matter. If you find a parking spot in an overcrowded parking lot and make your own makeshift space in an open area, have you seen cars immediately follow what you did? As soon as one person makes a move to do something different, others follow.

We incarnated to be 7 billion shepherds, not 7 billion sheep. We have become so obsessed with looking and acting like everyone else that we don't even know who we are anymore. Why do we constantly compare ourselves to others when we are *meant to be different?* Using others as our measuring stick is an exercise in futility. When we do this, we have lost the brightness of our own light: **our individuality.**

Because we are all unique, each one of us has an individualized perception of reality. No two people see the world in the same way. Just as though no two snowflakes are identical, there are no humans that are exactly alike. Even identical twins are not exactly alike physically, emotionally, and spiritually. They each have a unique perception and awareness. Each twin will still experience a different reality from the other.

We Are ONE

We are all interconnected with each other and with everything in existence. We are all from the same Source. Our God Force is our unique spark of divine light. When I use my healing gifts, I am expressing this God Force by assisting to reconnect persons back to this source energy, which is their true nature—their true essence. When I write, I am expressing my unique divine light by sharing my perception of how I see the world. I am able to express my true self, which brings me immense joy and passion for my work.

When enough people have awakened, we will have a great leap in vibrational frequency of the entire planet. Each of us as individuals is making a difference with our light. We are either contributing to the light of the planet or adding to the darkness.

Live Your Light

When we feel as though we need to conform to others' expectations, our bright light diminishes. Our life force gradually decreases as we blend into a sea of conformity. We are meant to be diverse. This is how we learn acceptance, tolerance, and compassion.

These are all attributes of love. It takes courage to be different and to speak out against the norm. It takes courage to live our life in accordance to our own personal truths, especially when they are different from what others believe.

Follow your heart and live your own truth. Have the courage to be your authentic self, without worrying about how you will be received by others. This is how to express your individuality. This is how you express your uniqueness, your spark of divine light. This is when your light is the brightest.

Accept yourself—love yourself, follow your passion, and allow your beautiful, God-given light to create a higher vibration across the globe for PEACE and UNITY. Only then, with this greater awareness, will we fully understand how barbaric we truly are with our hatred of people because they have different skin color, religious beliefs, and sexual orientation.

A barbaric society only knows war as a solution to conflict. An evolved society knows how to orchestrate a peaceful resolution to differences.

There are ultimately many opportunities for our unique God Force to be expressed. Our God Force is the spark of divine light that we carry from the source energy. *In all that we do, in every moment of our existence, we are expressing this God Force.* It is expressed in the work we choose, the actions we take, the choices we make, and through our emotions and judgments of each other.

We are the *oneness* of God manifest in form.

We are the *light* of God manifest in form.

We are the *energy* of God manifest in form

May you find your passion and awaken to your true self! Then all will come into balance. Your life will be more joyful! You will live in harmony and oneness with all that exists. This is LIFE. This is consciousness. This is an awakened soul.

Remember, Your Energy is Showing!

Live your Light,
Melissa

PEACE

Love and Light

Our pure essence is the frequency of love and light.
We spend our lives seeking our innate God Force of love and light.

NOTES

Introduction

1. Eric Pearl, The Reconnection: Heal Others, Heal Yourself (Carlsbad: Hay House, 2001).
2. Ibid.
3. Ibid.

Chapter 7

4. Rollin McCraty, Mike Atkinson, and Dana Tomasino. "Modulation of DNA conformation by heart-focused intention." HeartMath Research Center, Institute of HeartMath, Publication No. 03-008. Boulder Creek, CA (2003): 2.
5. Ibid.

Chapter 18

6. Wayne Dyer, Foreword, Anita Moorjani, Dying To Be Me: My Journey from Cancer, to Near Death, to True Healing (Carlsbad: Hay House, 2012), ix.
7. Anita Moorjani, Dying To Be Me: My Journey from Cancer, to Near Death, to True Healing (Carlsbad: Hay House, 2012), 113.
8. Ibid., 114
9. Ibid., 27.
10. Ibid., 114.
11. Ibid., 115.
12. Ibid., 115.
13. Ibid., 76.
14. Ibid., 145.
15. Ibid., 137.

Chapter 20

16. Masaru Emoto, The True Power of Water: Healing and Discovering Ourselves (New York: Atria, 2005), 12.
17. Ibid., 12.
18. Ibid., 12.

Chapter 21

19. http://www.harvardprostateknowledge.org/
    pomegranate-juice-may-slow-prostate-cancer-progression
20. http://www.fda.gov/ICECI/EnforcementActions/WarningLetters/
    ucm202785.htm
21. http://articles.mercola.com/sites/articles/archive/2012/03/07/fda-says-wal-
    nuts-are-drugs.aspx
22. Ibid.
23. http:www.fda.gov/iceci/enforcementactions/warningletters/umc202825.htm
24. http://thewallachfiles.com/here-is-congressman-ron-pauls-magnificent-
    floor-speech-introducing-the-health-freedom-protection-act/

Chapter 22

25. http://www.finance.senate.gov/imo/media/doc/111804sktest.pdf
26. http://www.lifeextension.com/Magazine/2012/10/
    The-FDA-Exposed-An-Interview-With-Dr-David-Graham/Page-01
27. http://vioxxnationalclassaction.ca/Press/2004_11_06_Lancet.pdf
28. Ibid.
29. http://www.finance.senate.gov/imo/media/doc/111804sktest.pdf
30. http://www.pbs.org/now/transcript/transcriptNOW101_full.html
31. http://www.lifeextension.com/Magazine/2012/10/
    The-FDA-Exposed-An-Interview-With-Dr-David-Graham/Page-01
32. http://vioxxnationalclassaction.ca/Press/2004_11_06_Lancet.pdf
33. Ibid.
34. http://www.bloomberg.com/news/articles/2011-11-22/
    merck-agrees-to-pay-950-million-to-settle-u-s-government-s-vioxx-probe
35. http://vioxxnationalclassaction.ca/Press/2004_11_06_Lancet.pdf
36. http://www.bloomberg.com/news/articles/2011-11-22/
    merck-agrees-to-pay-950-million-to-settle-u-s-government-s-vioxx-probe
37. http://www.lifeextension.com/Magazine/2012/10/
    The-FDA-Exposed-An-Interview-With-Dr-David-Graham/Page-01

Chapter 26

38. http://www.sciencedaily.com/releases/2011/08/110828101806.htm
39. Ibid.

Chapter 27

40. Norman Cousins, Anatomy of an Illness: As Perceived by the Patient (New York: W. W. Norton & Company, 2005).
41. Ibid.

Chapter 30

42. http://watson.brown.edu/costsofwar/
43. http://www.nejm.org/doi/full/10.1056/NEJMra010852